ForeWord Magazine 2005
Book Of The Year Award Winner

"Every Holocaust story is unique, but Joe Pell's is so extraordinary it transcends the genre. Pell's book is part World War II saga, part adventure tale, part memoir. It encompasses the tragedy of the war and the triumph of the survivors. It goes from Pell's days sleeping on leaves and digging for potatoes in the Ukranian woods to his life among the Bay Area's most successful business-men. It's also a great read."

—Caroline Jones
San Francisco Chronicle

"Although there are many holocaust memoirs, the stories of those brave men and women who fought back with the partisans is often overshadowed by stories of those who fled or survived the concentration camps. Joseph Pell's story is an especially compelling one not only because of his heroic actions in the face of the Nazi juggernaut and the rampant and often lethal Ukranian and Polish anti-Semitism, but it is an American immigrant success story as well."

—Michael Krasny
KQED Forum

Taking Risks

A Jewish Youth in the Soviet Partisans and His Unlikely Life in California

JOSEPH PELL
FRED ROSENBAUM

Western Jewish History Center
of the Judah L. Magnes Museum
Berkeley, California

RDR Books
Berkeley, California

Taking Risks

RDR Books
2415 Woolsey Street
Berkeley, CA 94705
Phone (510) 595-0595
Fax: (510) 228-0300
E-mail: read@rdrbooks.com
Web site: www.rdrbooks.com

and

Western Jewish History Center
of the Judah L. Magnes Museum
Berkeley, California

ISBN: 1-57143-116-0
Library of Congress Control Number: 2004095636

Copyeditor: Bob Drews
Cover and Text Design: Sara Glaser

Distributed in Canada by Jaguar Distribution
c/o Fraser Direct
100 Armstrong Way
Georgetown, Ontario L7G5S4

Distributed in the United Kingdom and Europe
by Roundhouse Publishing Ltd.,
Millstone, Limers Lane, Northam,
North Devon EX392RG
United Kingdom

Printed in Canada by Transcontinental Printing

To the memory of the family I lost.
For the future of the family I have.

JP

Table of Contents

Foreword

ON THE EVE OF THE HOLOCAUST, the photographer Roman Vishniak took a series of extraordinary pictures of Polish Jews. Looking at those photographs from that vanished age, we see a community of enormous complexity: urban and rural, religious and secular, young and old. It was a community in ferment as communists argued with Zionists and both argued with their traditionalist parents. As Jews acquired modern education for the first time, many revolted against their age-old status and sought new horizons. They embraced Hebrew and Polish alongside their *mama-loshen*, Yiddish. They moved from towns to cities, and some moved even further: to the West or to Palestine.

But these new horizons were often obscured by storm clouds. The Polish state, newly independent after World War I, awakened nationalist fervor that was frequently accompanied by anti-Semitism. Polish nationalists envisioned an ethnically pure Poland in which the Jews—ten percent of the population—would have no part. It was the ominous threat of this growing anti-Semitism

that gave urgency to the internal Jewish debates over Zionism, Bundism, territorialism, and communism.

The reverberations of these debates were felt in the countryside even as Jews continued much of their traditional lives, serving as the traders, artisans, and merchants for the Polish peasantry. Here, many Jews lived close to the land, almost peasants themselves. Vishniak's photographs captured these rural Jews and thus preserved for us the memory of a different type of Jew from the stereotype of the weakly Yeshiva student: physically strong and able to defend himself in a sometimes hostile environment.

It was in this rural setting that Joseph Pell (then Yosel Epelbaum) was born and lived his formative years. His memoir paints a vivid portrait of Poland in the interwar period, especially how it was experienced in the countryside. For the historian, this is vital testimony that gives added complexity to the story of the Polish Jews. Pell tells the story of a youth who learned to live by his wits and who found physical activity more compelling than book learning, a useful corrective to the image we may have of the Jews of the shtetl.

Indeed, it was these qualities—some innate and some learned—that helped the author survive the Holocaust, even as he lost his family. Here, we come to the most dramatic sections of this memoir in which Pell miraculously survives the betrayal of his family to the Nazis, escapes to the forest, and joins the partisans. Few accounts of the partisans can compete with the story told here. Pell's brigade protected families as well as fighters and, thus, he not only saved himself by taking up arms against the Nazis, but also contributed to saving others. The war that the partisans fought was not a pretty business and at times required harsh measures. Pell does not shrink from describing these measures, while graphically portraying the conditions that made them necessary.

Unlike many Holocaust memoirs, this one does not end with the war and this is precisely one of its strengths. How the survivors rebuilt their lives and what they took from their experiences are subjects that ought to be as interesting as their wartime experiences themselves. Pell gives us an unflinching account of his activities in the black market in Germany immediately after the war and also of his highly successful career as a real estate developer in the San Francisco Bay Area after he came to the United States.

In his postwar accounts, we see great continuities with the intrepid boy in prewar Poland and the partisan during the war: the ability to take risks, act on intuition, and operate almost instinctively in unfamiliar surroundings. The hilarious story of how, after coming to San Francisco, he bought an ice cream shop without knowing how to make ice cream is a priceless vignette that shows the way a shrewd immigrant could seize an opportunity and thus figure out how to make it in America.

This memoir is, then, not only a story out of the Holocaust, as important as that episode was in the life of Joe Pell. It is, in fact, much more sweeping, taking us from the Polish countryside to postwar Germany and America. It tells a story at once unique—because it is one man's experience—but also emblematic of major themes in twentieth-century Jewish history. Through this life, so passionately told, we gain invaluable insight into some of the secrets of modern Jewish suffering and survival.

David Biale

Prologue: Manievich in Nazi-Occupied Ukraine

September 3, 1942

MY INSTINCTS TOLD ME this was the day they would come for us. Disaster always seemed to strike on a Friday. Was it because they knew Jews would be at home preparing for *Shabbes?* Such were the fears that haunted me at the age of eighteen.

At about five in the afternoon I was in the backyard of our decrepit dwelling, hanging a pair of pants on the clothesline. First I heard the roar of motorcycle and truck engines. A moment later a bullhorn pierced the air like a gunshot: *"Juden raus, Juden raus."* It sounded like it came from just in front of our doorway.

Sensing a large force of raiders entering the house, I raced to the barn, about thirty yards away. I couldn't go back to check on my sick mother and my older brother, Sol. I couldn't go back for food or clothing. I had expected or hoped for some warning, anything, that would allow at least a few hours to pack up and try to get away. But the bullhorn told me I had no time at all.

I scrambled up the ladder to the hayloft. At one end, where the pitched roof met the floor of the loft, I burrowed myself in a pile of hay. I lay without making a sound, without moving a muscle.

The tumult on the street rang in my ears. Mothers screamed the names of their children, who wailed in terror. Men let out cries of pain as they were struck by shouting Germans and their Ukrainian henchmen. And the blare of that bullhorn, *"Juden raus, Juden raus,"* kept going on and on. For about two hours it was pandemonium.

Just before dark it quieted down. Then someone entered the barn. I heard heavy footsteps as he climbed the ladder. Through the hay, I could make out a well-armed Ukrainian militiaman swinging a lantern. My heart beat wildly. If only I had a knife in my hands, I thought, I'd plunge it into his chest. He looked around for a long, long minute while my life hung in the balance. Then he went back down.

I continued to lie still for another hour and thought of how things had come to this. Almost three years earlier, Hitler had attacked my native Poland. Our family fled east, seeking refuge under the Soviets. But the German army eventually invaded the USSR, too, and overran our small Ukrainian town. Then came the mass murderers of the SS. Were we all going to die in this alien land?

Suddenly, a shuffling noise from the other end of the loft! Another person had been silently hiding in the hay the whole time. Oh, let it be Sol. Maybe somehow he hadn't been in the house when they came. Maybe he'd had some premonition and gotten to the barn ahead of me.

We had become so close in the horrific year just passed. Sol was idealistic, almost dreamy, and I loved him. His goal in life was to make *aliyah* and live on a kibbutz. We were in a nearby wheat field one evening, back in June 1941, when the Germans first bombed Manievich, and I remember him looking up at the sky and saying, "When this war is over, there will be a Jewish state."

All of these thoughts went through my mind in the instant it took to make out who was coming toward me in the darkness.

And when I realized it was not Sol but a complete stranger, my heart sank. Sol must have been caught, inside or in front of the house, and now, along with our mother, was on his way to a terrible death. The instantaneous decision I made to save my own life meant that I had to leave them both. It was something I would live with for the rest of my days.

The man, who got up across the attic, brushing hay off his body, was now linked by fate to me. We decided to wait in the barn until midnight and then try to reach the vast forest that began at the north end of town about half a mile away. Afraid of being seen on the streets even at that hour, we went through backyards, fields, and narrow alleys on all fours, crawling in the dark over dirt and animal shit. We arose to climb over walls and fences, but it's fair to say the way we got to the woods was on our hands and knees. Not until we entered the forest did we stand upright.

We ran deeper and deeper into the black woods. When we were out of breath, we walked almost the rest of the night. A little before dawn we collapsed on the ground. With nothing more than the light summer clothing I'd been wearing, I was utterly unprepared for the rigors of the forest.

But I kept alive, joined a band of partisans, and fought back.

Many times in my life I've been in danger and somehow survived, even thrived. Usually it wasn't the result of long, deep philosophizing but, rather, quick thinking and then action. And I needed a lot of luck along the way, too.

My life has been one of extremes. I've known luxury but also have had to scrounge for potatoes to keep from starving. Much happiness has come my way and yet nothing can make up for what I lost. And for all my daring and independence, I'm actually quite shy. I have even been of two minds about telling this story; most of the time, I've wanted to keep it locked inside me.

ONE

Butcher's Boy

ONE OF MY EARLIEST MEMORIES is walking down a side street heading toward the river. I was nine. Even though it was Shabbes I wanted to go swimming. My father was known by all as a kosher butcher—it was part of his name, Hershel the Katzav—and he would be shamed if one of his five children was seen desecrating the Sabbath. So I wore my best trousers over my trunks, making it look like I was just out for an afternoon stroll.

From the bridge over the broad, blue Krzna River, no one seemed to be around. I slipped off my pants and looked down. Although I didn't know how to swim, I jumped in. I thought I was in shallow water, but it was over my head. Flapping my arms and churning my legs, I came to the surface, straightened myself out and started swimming.

Someone saw me leap off the bridge into the water that day and told my father. He was furious and called me a *goy*. There was nothing I could say. It pained me that I had hurt him so deeply, because he was a good man and I loved him. But even as a young boy I realized we were worlds apart.

I grew up in the late 1920s and 1930s in Biala Podlaska, in the province of Lublin in central Poland. In America virtually no one has ever heard of my birthplace. It's difficult to pronounce and even more difficult to remember. One family that immigrated to California from my town told people they came from the bigger and better-known Bialystock, eighty miles to the north, in a different province, and, except for the first few syllables of its name, a city with no connection to Biala Podlaska.

Yet Biala Podlaska was not small or insignificant, and anything but dull. Situated on a major railway line, it was a lively town of almost twenty thousand, with over a third of its residents Jews. In the center was a square lined with chestnut trees and various shops. I can still remember the jewelry stores with their glittering merchandise. Some distance away was a delightful private park. One had to pay something to get in, but we kids usually just climbed over the fence. Beyond it the countryside began with its sweet-smelling orchards and hayfields. Our little city had an airplane factory, hospitals, several Polish and Yiddish newspapers, and even a movie theater.

But it was the gigantic marketplace on the outskirts of Biala Podlaska that generated the most excitement. Beginning at daybreak every Thursday throughout the year, regardless how cold or rainy, thousands of peasants with their horse-drawn wagons would descend upon a vast, open field, turning it into a beehive of commercial activity for Jew and non-Jew alike. There, among many hundreds of vendors, each occupying the same small spot every week, you could find any type of food and clothing, and all manner of household items. The produce of the countryside was exchanged for the goods of the town. A farmer would sell his berries, turnips, or chickens. Before going home he would buy a dish or a tablecloth, or perhaps even a pair of shoes or a dress for his wife. But it wasn't all cold commerce: you could have your picture taken, watch a traveling circus act, or learn your future from a gypsy fortuneteller. And the colorfully costumed gypsies, whom everyone said were dangerous thieves, made the market even more thrilling for me. All week I looked forward to Thursday.

At the age of twenty-two, my father, Hershel Epelbaum, a serious Yeshiva student, married my mother and quickly began raising a family in Biala Podlaska. Sima, a daughter born before World War I, was their first child. Then they had four sons: Simcha was born around 1915; Sol soon after World War I; then me, Yosel, in 1924; and finally Moishe, my little brother, in 1930. My birthday, I think, was May 5. I don't know for sure because we never had any birthday parties; there just wasn't enough money or time for that sort of thing.

I lived with my parents, sister, and three brothers in an apartment at Ulica Yatkova 14, an appropriate address since in Polish it means Street of the Butchers, though our shop was at a different location. Our family of seven occupied one of four units in a plain two-story building. My mother's sister and her husband, a house painter, and their two daughters lived across the hall, while other relatives lived in the building next door. Our second-floor apartment today would be called a "large one-bedroom." It had a wide foyer, kitchen, living-dining room, and a good-sized bedroom. Fortunately it had a spacious attic, too, entered by climbing a narrow ladder in the stairwell between the two upstairs units. In that attic all four families in the building stored a thousand and one different things.

Although we were not far from the center of town, we had enough land behind our building to grow vegetables and even have a barn with cows, sheep, and horses. We constantly went into the nearby countryside looking for large and small animals to buy. So our everyday experience was more rural than urban.

It was only two generations ago when I was growing up in prewar Poland, but it could have been separated by a thousand years from the life I lead now. Daily existence required much effort. There was no plumbing, which meant that while we had basic chamber pots, we lacked real indoor toilets. Everyone in our building and the one next to it shared a crude wooden outhouse twenty yards behind our home. To get to it, you had to walk down two flights of stairs and around to the back of the building, even in the pitch-black night or in frigid temperatures. Our toilet paper was old newspapers that we cut up beforehand. Once a month or so the human waste was hauled off at night by Polish peasants who used it for fertilizer, but sometimes it rose so high that it came up through the hole in the wooden seat; it had to be tamped down before the toilet could be used. Of course, all of this seemed natural to me since I didn't know of anything else.

More of a problem was that all of our water for cooking and washing had to be pumped up from a communal well a block away and brought home in buckets. To keep the pump from freezing in the winter we insulated it with bundles of straw. Any water spilled near the well in cold weather turned into a patch of ice, and with a heavy bucket in your hand it was easy to slip and fall.

There was no electricity, so we read in the evening by the light of kerosene lamps, which had to be constantly filled and their wicks regularly replaced. Lacking refrigeration, we had to lay in a steady supply of ice in the cellar. We didn't have a radio or a telephone. Our stove was made out of hard clay, and we placed the pots and pans on simple, iron-rimmed openings in the stovetop over a wood-burning fire, wood that had to be chopped every few days and brought into the house. For heating, we put lumps of coal, or bricks of pressed, black peat moss, into a large oven that extended from floor to ceiling and stood at the intersection of the living room, kitchen and bedroom. Attached to this heater was a long, smooth bench of stone or plaster allowing us on cold nights to sit and warm our backs.

We'd get new coats and pants every third year before Passover. The tailor would come to the house to fit us, and it was an endless process since he might have to make as many as five visits in all. First, he took the measurements, the next time he'd deal with the shoulder padding, and then he'd bring the whole thing stitched together with white thread for a fitting. Often my mother would make him take it back for further alterations.

It was just as complicated with the shoemaker. We would select the leather, the sole, and the heel separately and then he'd make the shoe by hand. We could look through the window of his shop and watch week by week how our shoes progressed. Sometimes we got tall boots that were more fashionable than shoes, but they fit so tightly it would take half an hour of jumping around to get into them. To take them off, you had to put the heel into a wooden contraption, brace it with your other foot, and often still need someone else's help. But the day you finally were handed your new clothes, shoes, or boots was more joyous than any holiday.

If one of us was ill, he or she didn't see a real doctor but rather a kind of paramedic known as a *feldsher*. Ours was a jolly fellow from the neighboring town of Kobrin. We called him simply the Kobriner. Although he was able to write prescriptions, he usually preferred to administer a treatment known as *bankes*. For almost every disease we had, he or someone in our family would apply about a dozen or more small glass cups (bankes) to the ailing person's back. First a cotton wad on a wire was dipped in kerosene, lit with a match, and put into the cup to create a vacuum. Then the cup would be quickly clapped on the skin. This drew blood to the surface and was thought to release impurities and unblock congestion. I had my doubts even then that bankes had any positive effect beyond the psychological. The uncomfortable red welts left by this method were all too real, however. They would remain for four or five days. Whether dental care was as primitive I don't know because the only time my mother ever took me to a dentist I became so fearful in the waiting room that I ran off, never to return.

And I rarely traveled out of town. There was a bus that stopped daily in the main square and went on to Warsaw. But I never rode the bus or the train. Biala Podlaska and its surrounding countryside were my whole life.

Growing up, I felt closest to my big brother Simcha. He was tall and strong and very popular among the boys and girls in town. He had good business sense and worked hard to help support the family. Sima, more than a decade older than I, helped our mother run the household. Sol would be my closest companion later, when we worked in a factory under the Nazi occupation. And little Moishe—I still recall his bassinet swinging in the living room—was probably the smartest of us all. We called him *Mamzer*, in his case meaning someone shrewd beyond his years, though literally the term refers to a child born of an illicit sexual union. Later, at the tender age of ten, he would play a vital role in helping our family during the war. There was a sixth child, too, but she did not survive infancy.

My mother, born Rivka Goldszmit, from the nearby village of Yanova, was a quiet, gentle soul. An arranged marriage brought her together with my father. While raising the family and running the business, my parents worked together as a team, and there was little outward passion or affection. My father's mother lived with us too. She died when I was about four. I remember *Bubbe's* big trunk in which she kept her wigs and the many *chippiks*, the ornaments that decorated them.

How did we all sleep in two rooms? In the foyer, Sol slept in a common device known as a *shluf-banke*, basically a big wooden box. During the day it functioned as a chair or table. You could sit on it, work on it, and even prepare food on it. In the evening he would remove the wooden top and it became a bed; the mattress was just a burlap bag stuffed with straw. My sister Sima and my grandmother each had narrow beds in the living room where Simcha also slept on a convertible sofa bed. In the bedroom, little Moishe and I slept along either side of my father, head to toe, the three of us in the same bed. Nearby my mother had a bed of her own. In the morning, after our parents awoke and left the house, Moishe and I sometimes had pillow fights in our father's bed. More than once, the pillowcase broke, letting fly a torrent of feathers all over the bedroom.

But this kind of levity was rare, and none of us stayed in the house too long. We all had work to do and it revolved around the family business—purveying kosher meat. We drove our wagon out to the villages encircling Biala Podlaska, bought animals from the peasants, took the livestock back to town, had it ritually slaughtered, and then marketed the meat in our butcher shop.

We also had several cows for milking that we kept in our barn; we sold the milk and also made cottage cheese and yogurt. Sometimes we went into the fruit business, buying entire orchards "on the bloom." After the harvest, we'd sell as much fruit as we could and then can the rest, or press it into juice, storing it in our cellar and vending it in the winter. In the late summer, using fifty-gallon barrels we kept in the attic, we made pickles and sauerkraut that would last half the year.

But most of all we sold meat. I recall waiting for hours on Friday afternoons on the main road into town for my father to return with animals he'd purchased. When he finally appeared, I'd hop on his wagon to get an early glimpse at what he was bringing home—a couple of sheep, a calf, or a few geese.

About the age of ten I began going on those buying trips to the countryside with my oldest brother, Simcha. How I loved those outings! At dawn I would get the horse and wagon ready. We took a lot of pride in that wagon, with its steel axles and wheels and spokes of hard oak. The sides, with molded wood and iron rails, gave it a stylish look that set it apart from the other horse-drawn carts. The two of us would set out and ride for hours on the narrow, dirt roads, often lined with tall trees. We felt at home amidst the meadows, pastures, and orchards that we passed. We breathed deeply of the fresh country air.

Reaching the first of several hamlets we would visit that day, we'd ask if anyone had any livestock for sale. Although everything was bought after haggling, the process began even before we met the seller. If my brother spotted a familiar wagon from Biala Podlaska in the village, he'd likely hide ours behind a house or a stand of trees; he didn't want another buyer to follow us and make a rival bid. Only after our competitor left the area would we knock on the farmer's door and see the animal he had for sale. At times a bidding war was unavoidable. But Simcha was shrewd then too. Occasionally other buyers would pay him off just so he'd go away.

When we found an animal we wanted to buy, the bargaining became intense. The peasant needed every bit of money he could get to buy clothing and other goods for his family. And because profit margins were so narrow, we were not inclined to pay a zloty more than we needed to. I suppose it resembled an Arab bazaar. We would learn the cost from a farmer, shake our heads and walk away, knowing that we'd come back later. When it was finally time for serious negotiations, buyer and seller would arrive at the price through the noisy East European ritual of slapping the palms of each other's right hand. The farmer would state how much he wanted and Simcha or I would clap the man's hand hard, as if to register the amount. Then we would say how much we were willing to pay, and the peasant would bang one of us on the hand. Because we were always far apart at first, it took many rounds of vigorous claps to make a deal. Then, when we finally reached an agreement, we shook hands instead of clapping. A busy day always meant a sore, red hand by nightfall. Perhaps without the pain inflicted by this process, the bargaining would have gone on forever.

This was the only "business school" I attended—trading cattle in remote Polish villages with Simcha. I learned the law of supply and demand, the art of negotiating, the importance of timing, and also the need always to keep in mind the other fellow's situation. Was he really intent on selling? And what was he trying to accomplish? Was he strapped for cash? Did he want to trade one animal for another, or for something else?

I also developed a knack for assessing value, accurately estimating by sight and especially by touch the meat and the fat content of an animal. This was crucial since we put so much effort into finding the beast, negotiating for it, bringing it home (which in the winter meant hauling it by sled on the ice), butchering it, and then selling it at a profit.

One success still stands out in my mind. We knew that a farmer had an enormous bull for sale, weighing perhaps fifteen hundred pounds, the biggest in the entire region. As usual, we hid until we saw another potential buyer leave. We didn't want him to bid up the cost, nor did we want a partnership on this deal. In the end we bought the animal at a good price, but taking it home was something else again. The bull was not only huge but also wild. We needed a pole attached to the ring in his nose to keep him at bay. This was difficult enough, but then we had to cross a river by means of a small, floating platform called a *prom*, drawn by pulleys from each bank. Keeping the kicking bull under control in such tight quarters was almost impossible, but we somehow made it to the other side. When we got back to the main square of Biala Podlaska with our prize—it was just a few days before Rosh Hashanah—we were hailed like conquering heroes. Many in the town were familiar with that farmer and his giant bull, and that two of Hershel the Katzav's sons had bought it was big news. Getting a *metziah*, a bargain, gave me a great flush of excitement. And during all the decades that followed, I've never grown tired of that special feeling that comes from knowing I got a good deal.

Still, we struggled financially and lived week to week. My father had no real savings, just some spare cash in his pocket. Every Friday, to comply with the prohibition of carrying money on the Sabbath, he hid his small sack of zlotys in a secret compartment in a corner of the bedroom ceiling. To cover our expenses, he sometimes had to borrow money from a private lender, signing short-term promissory notes called *wechsels*.

Fortunately, because we were in the food business, we always ate well. The Shabbes dinners were especially delicious, and there was plenty to go around. Preparations for the Friday evening meal began on Thursday when my mother or sister would pick out a carp at the marketplace and bring it home, still alive, in a container of water. I would help the two women of the house as they made the traditional main course—gefilte fish. Literally "filled fish," this elaborate dish bears no resemblance to the "gefilte fish" that comes in a jar and can be purchased in any American supermarket.

First they took the carp out of the water and cut off its head. It still jumped around on the table, but after it slowed down, they would cut it into slices about three quarters of an inch thick. Leaving the skin of each section intact, they would remove the meat of the fish. Onions, eggs, starch such as crumbled-up hallah or matzah meal, and seasonings would be added to the carp flesh. Then they would carefully put the skin back on to look like the original fish. Even the head would be filled in this manner but my father was the only one who got to eat that part; he was served one half on Friday evening and the other on Saturday afternoon.

All the ingredients had to be finely chopped. Since we had no grinder, it all had to be done by hand with a heavy cleaver on a wooden block. This was my job, to *hock,* or chop, and it could last up to two hours. As I began chopping on Thursday evening, I could hear through our open kitchen window the sound of hocking throughout the entire neighborhood. Every family was chopping at the same time, and it was music to my ears.

Meanwhile, my mother and sister cooked the fish bones, along with carrots, onions, and spices in a pot of boiling water. Each piece of filled carp would be dipped in this mixture to prevent it from sticking. After the fish was cooked, it would be put on a deep serving platter and the simmering broth would be poured over the whole thing. A few hours later the juices would congeal into a jellied topping.

And this was just the main course. We also braided and baked our own hallah and made honey cakes and other sweets. With so many kids in the house, my mother had to keep these delicacies out of our reach or they would be gobbled up before Shabbes. We had a *shrank* in the living room, a free-standing closet that today you might call by the fancy name armoire, and they put the baked goods on top of that. More than six feet off the ground, it was a good spot, my mother thought, figuring I was too short even using a chair to reach so high. But sometimes I leaned the chair against the shrank and stood, precariously, on the top rung of the chair's back in order to bring down one of the treats. I was lucky not to break my neck.

On Friday mornings my mother and sister started preparing *kishka*, the meal we would have the next day, on the Sabbath afternoon. First they would select a foot-and-a-half-long piece of the widest part of an animal's stomach or intestine. After cleaning and scraping it well, they'd sew up one end with thread. Against that sewn end they'd push in the stuffing—flour, onions and lots of fat—so that as they worked, the inside lining of the kishka became the outside. It was like turning a giant sock inside out by pushing in the toe. Then they'd sew up the other end and put the kishka on top of the *chulent*, a big stew of meat, potatoes, and carrots. In order not to break the commandment prohibiting cooking on the Sabbath, I would carry the whole thing in one big pot across the street to the Piekarnia bakery on Friday afternoon and have them put it in their huge oven, still hot from the day's baking. There, along with the Shabbes meals of dozens of our neighbors, it would simmer overnight. When we retrieved it on Saturday and opened the pot for the festive midday meal, it was almost as if the kishka was crying; there was so much fat that you could see it coming through the skin. Of course in those days no one knew anything about cholesterol. If you ate fat you thought of yourself as being rich.

Passover was an even bigger production. It began more than a month in advance. We gave the house a thorough spring cleaning from top to bottom, looked for insects, and changed all the dishes and cooking utensils, which, with great difficulty, we brought down from the attic by ladder. Our matzahs came from a special bakery where each family made a reservation for the baking of its unleavened bread over a two-day period. When it was our turn my mother made sure to be there to observe the entire process whether there was a rabbi to oversee it or not. Finally the round matzahs—they looked like today's thin pizza crusts—were placed in huge wicker baskets lined with white paper. A man from the bakery put a rope through the handles in the middle of each basket and carried them on his back one at a time to our house. About four and a half feet wide at the top, the baskets couldn't even get through our front or back doors, so we unloaded the matzahs outside.

In late winter we would buy two geese and spoon-feed them grain every day to fatten them up. By Passover they couldn't even walk and were enormous by the time we prepared them for our Seders and other meals throughout the holiday week. We made use of the goose fat too, cooking it with browned onions and *gribbelach*, the crisp bits that remained after rendering the fat. Then we spread this *shmaltz* on the matzah. It was the tastiest snack you could ever want.

I can still see my family sitting around the table for those big, savory Shabbes or holiday meals. My father, *Tateh* as I called him, sat at one end of the table, Simcha at the other. Usually we had a guest, an *oyrech,* or needy person, whom my father brought home from the synagogue. Tateh wore a long, dark coat and was never without his yarmulke. In the winter, icicles clung to his black beard as he walked into the warm house to usher in the Sabbath.

We kids loved the hearty food. But the truth is we couldn't wait for those meals to be over. We were bored by the prayers, even by the Passover Haggadah. We were eager to escape the four walls of our house, meet our friends, and enjoy the outdoors.

Whenever I was free from my chores, I biked, swam, kayaked, and skated—on wooden skates with metal blades that I made myself. Most of all, I loved soccer and played right forward on a team of both Jewish and Polish boys. The games were on Shabbes and, like my swimming jaunts, a little deception was necessary. I'd hide my soccer clothes somewhere outside the house, so that when I left for a "walk" after our midday meal my father wouldn't know where I was spending the rest of the afternoon.

It wasn't all athletics. I played a lot of chess too and was quite good at it. But I felt most comfortable out of doors. I had a farm boy's chores and enjoyed them. I milked the cows and loved the taste of the warm, foamy liquid that no one would think of drinking today because it wasn't pasteurized. I chopped wood in the cold mornings, drew water from the well, fed the animals in the barn, led them out to the communal pasture, and brought them back at the end of the day. I even broke wild horses that we bought from the peasants. I knew how to distract a horse with some hay, then grab him by the mane and jump right on him, riding him bareback. It was also my job to lead the horses to the blacksmith. I would hold up the horse's leg for the man while he would file the hoof and then nail on the shoe. And at a very young age I saw horses bred. Simcha took me to see the whole exciting process with the powerful animals reared up on their hind legs. Of course, I saw countless cows give birth and immediately begin to lick their newborn calves.

I even felt at home on the cold cement floor of the slaughterhouse. After an animal was killed by the *shochet*, the ritual slaughterer, I would assist him in skinning it. The hindquarters were hoisted up first and, as the animal was raised with pulleys, I would help pull the skin down and remove the fat, meat, and inner organs, usually with my bare hands. Others might have been queasy, but to me it was a beautiful moment of truth. At last I got to see what we had really bought in the countryside the day before. And there wasn't *any* part of the animal that we didn't use. The head, the feet, and the lungs, you name it. They were all consumed.

I was comfortable enough in the slaughterhouse even to play a prank or two. One day, after we skinned a huge bull, I asked a Polish boy to hold for a second the bull's penis that I had just removed—it was two and a half feet long—and then I ducked out of sight. I returned about ten minutes later to find the kid still holding it in his hands and with an unhappy, foolish look on his face.

TWO

Out of Place

I WAS A DIFFERENT PERSON ENTIRELY in school, where I was shy and felt I didn't belong. My generation of Jews was the first in Poland to have compulsory public education, but the school met in a church and the Polish boys taunted me on the street even before I got to class. *"Zydi, Zydi l' Palestina,"* they jeered, "Jews, Jews go to Palestine." This was a refrain Jewish youngsters heard all over Poland.

I was also picked on because of my physical appearance. Not only was I small for my age, but I also had a growth on my neck just under the right side of my jaw. Although nothing more than a deposit of fatty tissue, it was about the size of a bread roll. And that's what the kids called me, *Bulka*, or roll. Eventually my mother took me to the local Jewish hospital to have it removed, but the doctor didn't sew up the wound properly and it left a noticeable scar.

Whatever the reasons, I just couldn't concentrate in the classroom and wanted to be alone as much as possible. My grades were poor, and I left school when I was thirteen, never to return.

My experience at the *heder*, the Jewish school we also attended, was even worse. The *melamed*, or teacher, an old man who stank terribly, literally beat the Hebrew words into our heads. He wielded a whip with leather strands knotted at the ends. The slightest misbehavior or even a mistake in memorizing—everything was taught by endless repetition—resulted in painful blows of the *konchuk*, his cat o' nine tails. Tateh, displeased with my performance in the public school, was enraged when I refused to attend heder. He hired a tutor to come to our house and give me Hebrew lessons. But it was no use. I learned to sight-read the language but never developed the fluency I wish I had now. At the time, I simply didn't see the point of it all.

I was intensely proud of *being a Jew* especially since we were under constant attack by the Polish Catholics. Yet *Judaism* held such little significance for me that even my Bar Mitzvah was meaningless. Of course my father took me to the *shul* around the time of my thirteenth birthday. But my stage fright, lack of preparation, and bad attitude all resulted in a miserable display. It was all I could do to go up to the *bimah*, the platform in front of the Holy Ark, and mouth the words of my part. I showed hardly any skill or enthusiasm and let Tateh down. Maybe he had suspected that this could happen for he invited no relatives or friends to the occasion. There was just some vodka and cake after the services for the old men who were regular members of the *minyan*. I didn't even stay around very long; as soon as I could, I raced out the door. This was the last straw for my father who now gave up on me, saying I'd never amount to anything. He didn't have the time or energy to devote to my emotional problems, and he had no patience with my refusal to get a Jewish education.

We had what you could call a generation gap in our family, and one of the conflicts was over religion. Obviously the rift did not stem from any enlightened philosophical position on the part of us kids. None of us was university-educated and we were so superstitious that we'd return to the house if a black cat crossed our path.

But we refused to take on faith Jewish law and belief. Neither my brothers nor my sister showed the slightest interest in the Torah or Talmud, the cornerstone of my father's life. To me they seemed as if they were the most obscure and irrelevant writings in the world. I not only violated Shabbes without any qualms if I thought I wouldn't get caught, but also ate the tempting Polish sausages once in a while. The son of a respected kosher butcher, I ate kielbasa even on the solemn fast day of Yom Kippur, though my friends and I went into a deep cellar to do so. We figured that in case God did exist, he wouldn't be able to see us sin so far underground.

The laws surrounding *shechita*, ritual slaughtering, made little sense to me. Yes, the animal was killed with one swift cut to the jugular; that was probably the least painful way of doing it. And the shochet first shaved the area around its throat to ensure that not even a strand of hair would impede his razor-sharp knife. But before that, the beast was tripped, held down on the floor, and bound by its legs. So I often witnessed an eight-hundred-pound cow thrashing around in fear. In another part of the same slaughterhouse animals were killed, standing upright, with a stun gun to the head. Because they collapsed immediately, it seemed more humane to me. But the rabbis ruled that method unkosher and pronounced the meat from such animals *treyf.*

My siblings and I had too much respect for our parents to debate these issues with them. But Tateh and Mameh were wounded by our deeds, if not our words. It was one thing that we all failed to observe Jewish law and that none of us was learned in

*From left: Sima and Simcha with friends in
Biala Podlaska in the late 1930s*

the sacred texts. But on top of that, neither Sima nor Simcha, both
in their mid- to late twenties before the outbreak of the war, got
married. Instead they dressed up and went out on dates, to parties,
dances, and masked balls, often with each other's friends. Along
with Sol, who was in his late teens before the war, they had active
social lives despite my parents' disapproval.

Simcha was also sexually active. Of course, young, single people didn't live alone then. But he had some privacy bringing a girl
home during the day when most of us were out. He also strolled
with one or another of his girlfriends in the orchards and hayfields near the edge of town. Especially after the harvest the smell
was intoxicating, an aphrodisiac. Many young people went there
to make love. Snooping through Simcha's wallet, I would find
condoms that he bought in the drugstore without any problem.

The idea that you had to wait for marriage to have sex was another casualty in the war between the generations.

Sima, the oldest child, was dedicated to our parents. She helped Mameh cook and clean and nursed Tateh through his illnesses. He suffered from painful outbreaks of boils on his body, and my sister stayed up all night if necessary to apply hot compresses and lance the carbuncles. But it was a major source of disappointment for my parents that their attractive daughter remained single. Although the dowry they could provide was modest, this was not the reason she had not married by her late twenties. It was rather that she saw no shame in a single life. On the contrary, she loved going out on the town in a fashionable dress, sleeveless in the summer, and with her hair made up. And Sima was willing to wait for the right man to come along; she had no intention of rushing into marriage to please my parents or anyone else. My sister was a bit of a romantic, I suppose. With beautiful penmanship, she wrote in her diary almost every evening.

As for me, I flirted with girls but was too young and bashful to be seriously involved with the opposite sex. Anyway, I was drawn to nature more than to people, and it was hard for me to make friends, either with boys or girls. I was a loner. But like my sister and brothers, I was on a path completely different than Tateh.

It is not that my father was so rigid. True, he rose every weekday at 5 A.M., strapped on his *t'fillin*, the little black boxes containing holy words on parchment, and dutifully recited the morning prayers. But he often spoke proudly of his service in World War I, and certainly could not have kept kosher or observed Shabbes in the army of Czarist Russia, which ruled our part of Poland at that time and recruited its young men. Maybe in him there was a tiny bud of the rebellion that later bloomed in us. But having grown up in a small town in the late nineteenth century, he could not grasp the "youth culture" that my generation created in interwar Poland. His goal had been to marry and raise a large traditional Jewish family as soon as possible. We had other ideas. In fact, the whole concept of "youth"—involving sports, music, fashion, romance, and clubs—was foreign to him. And even if Tateh had wanted to indulge us a bit in our revolt, as one of the leading kosher butchers in town he had to be concerned about the opinions his religious customers had of his children.

The younger generation learned Polish in school or on the streets, and we tended to speak it among ourselves. My father knew a good deal of Polish, of course, and often used it in business, but he preferred Yiddish. So a linguistic division arose between the generations as well. I literally talked to my sister and brothers in one language and to my parents in another.

But what really put my father on the defensive was his difficulty in making a living. Although all of us worked hard, we never seemed to get ahead. It was toughest on my mother, who not only ran the household but also toiled in the family business. I recall her sitting in our butcher shop, waiting for customers to come in on a wintry day. She had to leave the door wide open so people would not think we were closed and patronize another store. To keep herself from freezing, she set a bucket of hot coals on the floor under her skirt. Her parents had been jewelers and were a bit better off than us, so Mameh wasn't cut out for such a difficult life.

She rarely complained, but Simcha loudly criticized Tateh for our bad economic situation. The oldest son put in longer hours than any of us and often expressed his frustrations at the dinner table. He felt stuck in the role of breadwinner because of our father's lack of success. Pointing to little Moishe, he even blamed Tateh for having more children than he could properly support.

And, because the anti-Semitic government in Warsaw passed

a series of laws in the late 1930s intended to hurt the Jews economically, we suffered even more. Kosher butchers were singled out for especially cruel punishment. We were accused of trying to monopolize the nation's market (an absurd charge since non-Jews seldom came into our stores), and severe limits were put on the amount of kosher meat we were allowed to sell. Simcha opened a small non-kosher butcher shop across town, and Sol chose not to go into the meat business at all. Instead, he helped support the family with his earnings as a cabinetmaker.

As for me, I was a boy happy to work in our family's business, especially as a buyer of farm animals. Yet Simcha worried that I would follow in his footsteps and remain in that dead-end job for the rest of my life. He urged me to learn a trade and set out on my own. But I did not follow his advice. The rough life I had, close to the earth, suited me fine. And anyway, I wanted to spend as much time as I could with Simcha.

There was one thing, however, that would have changed my direction in life. I would have made aliyah, immigrated to Palestine, if I could have obtained an immigration certificate. This was the great hope of most of the Polish Jews of our generation, especially after America closed its doors to us in 1924.

Zionism had a terrific appeal to the youth of Biala Podlaska, and most of us went around town collecting coins for Palestine in little blue and white boxes. As the attacks against Jews increased in the late thirties, and the economy worsened, we actually agreed with our enemies when they shouted, "Zydi, Zydi l'Palestina." The idea of a Jewish state, where we would work the land and control our destiny, filled us with pride. For many of us, Zionism, with its promise of a better life in the future, took the place of Judaism, which we felt belonged to the ancient past.

The ultra-religious Jews in town sensed this threat. The Hasidic sects, of which there were many in Biala Podlaska, openly criticized the Zionists. One rebbe even pronounced a *herem*, excommunicating the "atheistic" Zionists from Judaism. But traditional Judaism was on the defensive during these years and the rebbe's ban, which he issued with the blast of a ram's horn, was widely considered pathetic.

Even those like my father—"middle of the road" orthodox—were often sympathetic toward Jewish nationalism. After all, my aunt and uncle and their two daughters, cousins whom I played with as a small boy, made aliyah in 1932 and were given a joyous sendoff. So Palestine was hardly a remote possibility.

My sister and two older brothers were enthusiastic Zionists. But the movement was deeply split ideologically and they belonged to rival youth groups. Sima and Sol, both quiet types, were members of Hashomer Hatzair, an organization on the far left that stressed the agricultural life of the kibbutz and co-existence with the Arabs. Simcha, on the other hand, was a member of the militant Betar, the youth group of Vladimir Jabotinsky's Revisionist Party. Jabotinsky advocated a giant Jewish state on both sides of the Jordan River and saw no other way of achieving it than by armed force. All the Zionists urged Jews to be active and not passive, to decide their fate with their own hands. It's just that Jabotinsky told us to have something *in* our hands to make sure we'd succeed.

There were other Zionist youth groups, including religious Zionists. But the conflict between the Hashomer and Betar was particularly sharp. Simcha and Sol had many heated arguments about the best way to win Palestine for the Jews, and they each tried hard to recruit me. Eventually, I joined Betar not because I fully understood the political issues but because I was so influenced by Simcha. And I loved the smart, red-brown uniforms we wore as we marched in military formation through the town and into the countryside. When the Hashomer called us fascists and claimed that our "brown shirts" were appropriate garb, we shouted back that we wore the color of the earth of Palestine. We marked time in Hebrew: *"Echad, shteyem, shalosh, arbah."* (One, two, three, four.) We sang inspiring songs, held athletic events, and even trained with wooden rifles. I lived in an anti-Semitic society, but Betar gave me a lot of self-respect.

My favorite day of the whole year was Lag B'Omer in the spring, a minor Jewish festival but for us a joyous holiday celebrating both a victory over ancient enemies and the beauty of the great outdoors. Our procession on Lag B'Omer was led by the marching band of Maccabi, a Jewish sports group that had bought its instruments from a German army band based in Biala Podlaska during World War I. The whole town took notice of our parade. At one of the early ones, Polish kids threw inkwells at us as we passed under the windows of their high school, and then ran out to beat up several Jewish boys. But we were not afraid to fight back and, after that, they grudgingly let us march without incident.

In 1936, the charismatic Jabotinsky came to Brest-Litovsk, just over the Bug River about twenty-five miles east of Biala Podlaska. I remember cycling there with Simcha to hear him speak. A large hall was packed with admirers as he gave a long, fiery talk in Yiddish. The head of Betar in the late 1930s was his protégé, a young lawyer named Menachem Begin, and we heard him several times in Biala Podlaska itself. But we Betarniks were not content to let the Hashomer Hatzair hold their rallies. We harassed them every chance we could. One time a few overzealous Betar members released a powerful sneezing powder into the air at a Hashomer gathering and completely disrupted the event. Later, we were paid back with a barrage of rotten eggs.

Other Jews forcefully rejected both religious observance *and* Zionism and worked to promote Jewish cultural life in a Poland they hoped would become democratic and socialist. These were the Bundists, who maintained a good library and put on many plays and poetry readings in Yiddish. But sometimes they attacked one of the Zionist groups with their fists.

There were even Jewish anarchists in Biala Podlaska. But those considered most subversive by the authorities were the communists. You could get ten years in prison just for raising the red flag. Two older cousins on my father's side of the family, who lived downstairs from us, were party members and once hid some of their pro-Soviet literature in our apartment. We hated being put in danger in this way and felt that these *farbrente*, or fanatic communists, were misguided at the very least. But my parents also understood the appeal that the USSR, with its promise of class equality and an end to religious discrimination, held for Jews in these difficult times. The underground Communist Party wasn't large in Biala Podlaska, but about half its members were Jews.

Divided as we Jews were, every one of us lived under the dark cloud of Polish anti-Semitism. We were well over three million strong during my youth, about ten percent of the country's population. But it seemed we had few allies among the Poles and none among the Ukrainians, a minority group even larger than we were. The Polish nationalists accused us of being disloyal; the Church branded us as Christ-killers; and the peasants often suspected us as dishonest. It is true that President Jozef Pilsudski, who came to power in 1926, shielded the Jews to a degree. But he died in 1935, deeply mourned by Jew and non-Jew alike. Under the right-wing dictatorship that followed, we were utterly defenseless.

Maybe it was slightly better for Jews in my town than elsewhere in Poland. In Biala Podlaska, we could serve in the volunteer fire department, for example, and several Jews sat on the city council. But the number of Jewish officeholders fell with every election as time went on. And even though Jews made up a third of the town, the municipality allocated a mere pittance for our needs. Overriding everything was the fact that we never actually felt Polish; they never let us. It was as if we were part of another nation—the Jewish people—that fate had set down in this godforsaken place. Of course we interacted with Poles. We needed them and they needed us for business. But we never truly mixed, certainly not socially. As a youth in Biala Podlaska, I would never think of entering a church or even the home of a Catholic.

The Polish government faced critical problems in the late 1930s. Two giant, menacing powers, Nazi Germany and Soviet Russia, bore down on the country from each side. And the economy was in a shambles. Half the population still lived on farms plowed by horses or by hand. Yet the Polish parliament seemed obsessed with the Jews and, of all things, kosher slaughtering!

My family was stunned to see the lawmakers devote literally half of their legislative sessions between 1936 and 1938 to regulating the kosher meat industry out of existence. After holding a series of humiliating hearings filled with anti-Semitic slurs, the Seym, or parliament, passed laws phasing out shechita altogether. A complete ban was not scheduled to go into effect until the end of 1942 (when, as it turned out, the Polish government was no longer in existence), but even in the late 1930s they imposed a tight quota on the number of animals that could be ritually slaughtered. Every Jewish group, from the God-fearing Hasidim to the non-religious Bundists, loudly protested this outrage, a blow against freedom of religion, a slap in the face to all of Poland's Jews.

For the Epelbaum family it also meant a drastic reduction in

business and a mortal threat to our livelihood. We tried to cope
with the ridiculous rules the best we could. One way was simply
to sell non-kosher meat. This is why, beginning in 1938, Simcha
ran a little store in the Polish part of town. Out of respect for my
father he didn't sell pork.

In order to buy kosher meat for our main shop we frequently had to operate in secret. We would buy a sheep or calf from
a farmer right outside town and arrange to come back later to
slaughter it. The seller would usually be asleep when we brought
in the shochet, around midnight, to kill the animal according to
Jewish law. Then, still inside the peasant's barn, we'd cut up the
carcass within a few minutes and hide the pieces of meat under
our clothes for the long run back home. I could fit a leg or side
of lamb under my belt or inside my shirt. It was such a strange
sensation, that still-warm, freshly cut meat against my body as my
brothers and I tore through the dark fields and alleys. Because our
best customers had heard from us the day before that a shipment
was coming early the next morning we could quickly sell all the
meat before the police were onto us.

Beyond all of this, we had to cope with other economic obstacles put in the way of Jews that dated from the birth of the Polish republic after World War I. There were harsh penalties for
violating the Sunday Closing Law, for example, forcing business
that day to be conducted through the back door; someone always
had to be on the lookout for the police. We were also harassed by
government officials who arrived monthly to check our scales to
ensure we weren't overcharging people. They then made us pay an
exorbitant fee for the inspection.

Most of all we dreaded the tax collector. Not surprisingly, the
tax laws penalized small businessmen, who tended to be Jews.
Failure to pay resulted in the confiscation of your entire stock of

goods. A taxman once came into our store and brazenly hauled off a huge slab of beef. This triggered an explosion of rage in Simcha, who walked up behind him, hit him on the side of the head with the brass knuckles he often carried, and knocked him out cold. That particular tax collector never bothered us again, and Simcha was never identified as the one who assaulted him. But this sort of violence by Jews against Poles was rare. Almost always it was the other way around. If we ventured outside the Jewish section of town, we were always at risk of being beaten up by Polish hooligans.

There were some Poles who were sympathetic to our plight, among them peasants whom my father invited into our home on Shabbes. These were men who came into town on Saturday to deliver animals we had purchased during the week, and they often stayed to share our big midday meal or at least a drink of strong vodka. As they gathered around the table, Tateh would hit the bottom of the quarter-liter bottle—called a *czwartka*—with his fist three or four times to make the cork fly out. Even us kids would have a taste.

Our Polish guests were outwardly friendly, but even as a child I always felt uneasy by their remarks. They praised my family but as an exception among the Jewish race. *We* weren't the communists, swindlers, blasphemers that most Jews were; *we* were different. "And if trouble comes to Biala Podlaska," they said, referring to the pogroms in other Polish towns in the mid-thirties, that had left several Jews dead, they promised my father that they would protect *us*. "Don't worry, Hershko," I remember them saying with a smile as they downed their glasses.

Of course we would soon be without protection against a far greater calamity than a pogrom—the German invasion of Poland and the outbreak of World War II.

Tension increased throughout the spring and summer of 1939. Everyone sensed that Hitler's shrill demand for the return of the Free City of Danzig to Germany and the right to build a highway and railroad across the Polish Corridor would inevitably lead to war. In late July, Polish regiments were being called up for field exercises all around Biala Podlaska. In mid-August, my older brothers and I went down to the railroad station to watch departing draftees. As they waved from the trains and sang the national anthem, their faith in victory seemed unbounded. The cocksure Polish public thought that their soldiers, who had defeated the Red Army in a border war two decades earlier, could certainly counter a German invasion until help arrived from the western democracies. Moreover, this time the Soviet Union might be an ally. After all, Stalin had actively opposed the Nazis for years, and if he didn't send troops against them, surely he would provide the Poles aid and allow British and French forces to enter Poland through his territory.

But these illusions crumbled on August 22, with the announcement of the Soviet-German Nonaggression Pact that stunned the world. Now the threat Hitler might have faced from the east was neutralized. War could break out any day, it seemed, and Poland had never been more vulnerable.

During the last week of peace the suspense threw our lives off track; we had no idea what to expect. The opening of the school year was postponed across the country. Gold coins were bought when they could be found and hidden in backyards. Government records were boxed and transferred to what were considered safe villages. Municipal officials were ordered to cancel their vacations and prepare for the possibility of an attack as best they could. We heard rumors that people were abandoning Warsaw to avoid surprise bombings. Then, on August 30, we learned from posters pasted up throughout Biala Podlaska that a general mobilization would occur the next day, fewer than twenty-four hours, it turned out, before the German onslaught and far too late for the defenders to be properly deployed.

Because it had one of the few airplane factories in Poland, Biala Podlaska was bombed even before Hitler's army crossed the border. At about 3 A.M. that Sunday morning of September 1, 1939, planes pounded the town killing several people. At first light Simcha, Sol, and I viewed the extensive damage and returned home with a foretaste of the destruction that lay ahead.

Within days the Blitzkrieg, a kind of attack the world had never seen before, rolled rapidly across Poland and we became horrified at the prospect of a German occupation. We had learned of *Kristallnacht*, less than ten months earlier, through newspaper reports, and also heard firsthand accounts of the persecution of German Jews, because some of those deported to Poland had settled in Biala Podlaska. Now we received the news of atrocities committed by the Nazis as their panzer divisions overran northern and western Poland and headed for our region.

The advance of the Wehrmacht seemed unstoppable. It is often said of that war that Polish cavalry charged German tanks and I don't doubt it. But even though I was not on the battlefield, I witnessed problems faced by the Polish military that were even more serious. In the opening days of fighting, the country's communication and transportation systems were severely crippled by enemy dive-bombers. They knocked out so many bridges and railway lines that reservists had no way to get to the front. In Biala Podlaska we saw hundreds of infantrymen, in spotless uniforms, just milling around with no place to go. They were typical of almost five hundred thousand Polish troops—about half of the entire army—who never saw combat.

Although my two older brothers were of draft age, for some

reason they were never inducted. I don't know if they would have served. By this time no one in my family felt any loyalty to Poland or placed any trust in the judgment of its leaders. The government in Warsaw still issued patriotic, even boastful statements about repelling the invaders, but we all knew the war would be over in a matter of weeks.

Meanwhile, small knots of Jews gathered each evening in the main square, worriedly discussing what the Polish collapse would mean. Some of the older people urged calm. They reminded us that the German occupation of Biala Podlaska for three years during World War I hadn't been that severe. There had been some shortages, as well as strict curfews but, all in all, those who remained in town fared much better than those who fled east. Others, among the religious people, said that everything was in God's hands anyway, that our fate was *beshaert,* or preordained, and that we simply ought to wait.

My father was not reassured.

In the second week of September, a German tank entered the town and headed down Brisker, the main street. It soon left, though, so we assumed it was part of a reconnaissance patrol. Any moment, we thought, the full-scale occupying force would arrive.

Then, on September 17, two and a half weeks after the start of the war, came electrifying news: The Soviet Union had attacked Poland from the east and its army was moving in to save us. We didn't know it at the time, but this partition of our country had been agreed upon by Hitler and Stalin in a secret addendum to the nonaggression treaty the month before; in truth the Soviets were anything but liberators. To us, though, the only thing that mattered was that the next foreign soldiers we saw were wearing a red star on their uniforms. On September 26, a large column of Soviet troops took control of Biala Podlaska.

The Poles were downcast, but the Jews were filled with relief and almost giddy. We openly welcomed the Red Army, which included a considerable number of Jews, even among its officers. A big pro-Soviet parade was held, and Jews made up the large majority of the marchers. The Poles would never forgive us for our support of the invaders because Russia, after all, had occupied most of Poland for a century and a quarter until 1918. In the minds of our neighbors, the hero's welcome we gave Stalin's men proved that we had been disloyal to Poland all along, to say nothing of being godless communists. But the Poles were the ones who had made us feel like unwelcome strangers in a land we had inhabited for almost a thousand years. And, of course, they were not facing the same threat from Hitler and his SS that we were. For us the USSR was simply the lesser of two evils.

True, some of the Jewish communists, operating openly for the first time, rubbed the Poles' noses in their defeat. One young Jewish woman, proudly holding a red flag in her hand, stood in front of city hall and blocked the Polish mayor from entering. Other Jews informed the Soviet military commanders of Polish officials who had been the harshest anticommunists before the war. These unfortunates were now slated for deportation to the Siberian gulag.

There were bizarre moments, too. In a communist parade down the main street, a woman with one leg much shorter than the other limped along shouting in Yiddish, *"Alle gleich, alle gleich."* (All are equal, all are equal.) At fifteen, with a limited grasp of politics, I was thoroughly confused.

We spoke Yiddish with some of the Soviet soldiers and officers, making friends with them. Because the war had suddenly brought the economy to a standstill, the Red Army distributed black bread and other goods to the population. Especially cheered by the turn of events was my father. He was by no means a communist, and he also knew the kosher meat business was unlikely to recover under Stalinist rule. But he was one of the few Jews who had had good experiences while in the czar's army during World War I and never had a bad thing to say about the Russians.

Yet to our dismay, within a few weeks there were rumors the Red Army was moving out. We had thought that the new border would be the Vistula River, giving the Kremlin about two thirds of the country. The Soviets had actually advanced beyond us to the town of Mezritch, some ten miles to the west, and we expected them to go much further—all the way to Warsaw. But the secret agreement with the Germans gave the Soviets only the eastern *half* of Poland and made the frontier between the two superpowers the Bug River. This meant we were going to be on the German side by twenty-five miles! The Russians—no doubt wanting to see how much they could get away with—had gone too far. Now they were ordered to pull back.

At first the Soviet commander denied they were leaving, but at night we saw vehicles removing supplies and equipment. It soon became clear that the Bug would indeed be the border, and finally the Soviets themselves admitted as much.

To their credit, they offered to evacuate any Jews wishing to leave. They actually encouraged us to go with them, in a convoy of military vehicles, to Brest-Litovsk. There, we would be on the eastern bank of the Bug and in the first town within the true Soviet zone of occupation.

Now, like all the other Jews of Biala Podlaska, we had to make a grave decision. To go east with the Red Army was no easy choice. We would not only abandon our homes and businesses, but we also would probably be forced to become Soviet citizens and never be allowed back into Poland. Furthermore, there was always the

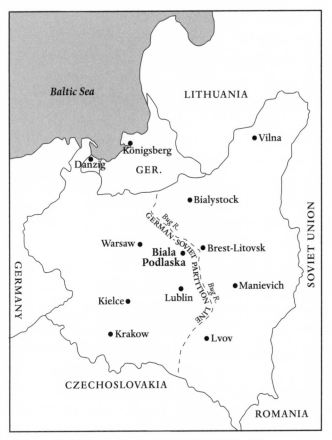

Poland after the outbreak of World War II

possibility of being sent to a labor camp deep inside Russia. My parents knew that Jewish observance would be difficult under Stalin, and we kids knew that Zionist activity was forbidden. And again we were reminded that those who went on the road during World War I suffered more than those who remained behind.

We had about a day to make up our minds. Tateh and Simcha, their faces drawn, huddled for hours and finally called us together and said we were leaving. More than anyone else in the family,

Simcha kept up with the news and was well aware of the Nazi record of persecution. He was fearful of what the Germans would do to us. And my father, of course, was somewhat favorable toward the Russians.

So the seven of us left Ulica Yatkova 14, the apartment where my parents had lived for almost thirty years and the only home I had ever known. We left behind our farm animals, including a spirited colt I was especially fond of, and our prized wagon. Since we owned no suitcases, we walked through the streets carrying our bedding and clothing in bundles tied with rope. There was no way to transport any furniture or even cooking utensils. The Poles, who quietly looked on as we trudged to the main square where the Red Army trucks were waiting, did not seem sorry to see us go.

Only six hundred Jews from Biala Podlaska went east with the Soviets, less than ten percent of the Jewish community. Nearly every one of those who remained would be murdered by the Nazis in the next few years, most of them gassed to death in Treblinka or Sobibor.

Of course none of us could know or even imagine the extent of the danger we were fleeing. We were grim and anxious that late October day in 1939 but not in a panic. We had had our disagreements over the years, but now each one of us sensed the importance of staying together as a family. Tateh surely expected to return to Biala Podlaska, even if it might take a while. He kept the keys to the house with him in a safe place.

THREE

Life under Stalin

CROSSING TO THE EASTERN BANK of the Bug River, we felt some relief in Soviet-occupied Brest-Litovsk, the nearby town we had visited before the war. The local Jewish community was under great pressure, but it did the best it could to help us, along with thousands of other refugees who had fled the Nazis and made Brest-Litovsk their first stop. The Red Army provided temporary housing.

But we soon became painfully aware of the hardships of life in a communist state. The Soviet administration prohibited the sort of free market trading, in animals or anything else, that had been our livelihood back home. There was strict rationing, and all goods were distributed through government-run stores that had long lines of people in front of them. The shortages were so great that we got in any queue we saw even if we didn't know what was for sale. Whatever it was, we figured we either needed it or could trade it to someone who did.

Simcha grew even more frustrated than the rest of us. He

bought cases of vodka on the black market and began to sell bottles for a profit. But it wasn't long before he was caught and jailed. I don't doubt that the police drank up the vodka they confiscated from him and had a ball. When my parents sought out one of the Jews among the high-ranking Soviet functionaries to intervene on Simcha's behalf, the official demanded vodka as a bribe!

Within a week my brother was released, but we soon had to deal with something far more threatening. The Soviets, faced with the influx into their zone of a quarter million Jews from German-occupied Poland, required that each refugee family choose between two fateful alternatives: the first was called "passportization" because it meant taking out Soviet passports and becoming full-fledged citizens of the USSR. There would be little expectation of ever returning home and we would likely have to spend the rest of our lives under communism. The second option was to remain resident aliens and hope to be repatriated after the war. But there was an immediate price to be paid for this choice—a trip deep into the frozen Russian interior. This is because those who declined the Soviet passports were shipped thousands of miles east to work in mines or factories.

Like most Polish-Jewish refugees, we decided not to opt for Soviet citizenship and anticipated a long, hard journey by train into the Asian part of Russia, possibly as far as Siberia. So, we never fully settled in Brest-Litovsk. For several months we sat around waiting for the order to evacuate. But the call never came. Due to an administrative mix-up—and these were commonplace in the USSR—we were overlooked and the trains for the east left without us. We thought we were lucky. We got to stay without having to accept the Soviet passports.

But the bitter irony of those terrible years was that you never knew what would save your life and what wouldn't. As it turned out, the Jews who worked for Stalin beyond the Ural Mountains did suffer greatly, but more than three quarters of them survived the war. Of those like us who remained in the Soviet-occupied zone of eastern Poland, over ninety percent would be killed.

While we stayed within the borders of what had been prewar Poland, we had to move one more time. The Red Army decreed that no refugees could reside as close as we were to the German frontier, so in early 1940 we were transferred about a hundred miles southeast of Brest-Litovsk to the small town of Manievich in the province of Volhynia.

We were among some five hundred refugees sent there, and with our arrival the Jewish community of Manievich doubled to about a thousand. There were perhaps another thousand non-Jews. The town's main feature was its proximity to the Polesie forests of northern Volhynia, several thousand square miles in size and one of the most thickly wooded areas in all of Europe. For this reason, Manievich was somewhat of a resort and for the first six months we were housed in an abandoned compound, with communal kitchens, originally built for recreational use. But much more important to the local economy were logging, milling, wood processing, and woodcarving. Volhynia possessed almost a third of all the timber resources of prewar Poland, and the native woods of oak, birch, pine, and ash were of the highest quality and in demand throughout the Continent.

The population here was different from that of central Poland where I had grown up. Although there were some Poles, two thirds of the Volhynians were ethnic Ukrainians. A large majority of them were illiterate and their standard of living was among the lowest in Eastern Europe. Most were plagued with alcoholism.

The Ukrainians were more hostile toward the Jews than the

Poles were. In Ukrainian Orthodoxy, the idea that the Jews killed Christ was even stronger than in Polish Catholicism. Ukrainian nationalism was fiercer, too. Unlike the Poles, they hadn't had a country of their own for many centuries. They had been dominated by the Russian czars, were forced to live under Polish rule between the world wars, and since 1939 were under the thumb of the most hated enemy of all—the Soviet Union. Desperate to hold onto their culture, religion, and small private farms—all targets of Stalin—the Ukrainians became obsessed with having a state of their own. They wanted to turn Volhynia into the northwestern part of the Ukraine, a new country whose capital would be the medieval city of Kiev.

They thought the Jews were poisoning their hopes. Because some Jews held high positions in the Soviet administration they saw us all as Bolsheviks working hand in glove with the Kremlin to frustrate Ukrainian national ambitions.

My family learned some Ukrainian, as well as a little Russian. Nonetheless, we were much more isolated than we had been in Biala Podlaska, or even Brest-Litovsk. We felt cut off from the world. Manievich sat on an important railway line, but travel without a Soviet permit was forbidden. Communist control of the economy tightened with every passing month in 1940, and private property was almost completely abolished. Small farms still functioned in the countryside but collectivization, everyone said, was fast approaching. My family, refugees with no business connections in this unhappy land, was very worried about economic survival.

Tateh's religious activities paled in comparison with the rich Jewish life he had led back home. The native Jews of Manievich were friendly, but their synagogues and other communal institutions had been dismantled. My father went to Shabbes services in a small minyan held in someone's home so as not to attract attention. Because of our difficulty obtaining food, Sabbath and holiday meals were nothing like the feasts we had enjoyed in Biala Podlaska. In Manievich my brothers and I even resorted to eating treyf in the house. Sometimes we took a thick slice of pork fat, fried it with onions and then poured in eggs that puffed up two inches high. Although my parents were disgusted by what we did, they decided not to stand in the way of their hungry children. They simply left the house during such meals.

This was an edgy period of waiting; we all had too much time on our hands. Simcha, not surprisingly, had a girlfriend he saw every day. But none of us had the social life we had enjoyed in Biala Podlaska. All of the Zionist youth groups were shut down by the authorities, as were most of the Jewish newspapers, cultural organizations, and sports clubs. We could not make a living, pursue our interests, or even legally travel to the next village.

Little Moishe, now ten, was a great joy to us. He was the only one in the family "in business" while we were in Manievich. Because he was so young, he aroused no suspicion on the trains as a smuggler. The Soviet distribution system, always poor, had broken down completely by 1940, and it was common for entire towns in our region to lack basic commodities such as matches, soap, or sugar. We would find out where the shortages were and send Moishe with the badly needed goods. He was usually successful, coming home with a pile of rubles or with items that were in short supply in Manievich or another town where he could sell them. One night, after an especially productive run, he put his gains on the table and, with a smile, told his three unmarried older brothers: "Guys, I can make enough to support a wife."

For a while I had a part-time job of my own, loading sacks of potatoes. Occasionally, I could steal a bag and bring it home to the family. But we all knew that we couldn't go on like this much longer.

Then, in early 1941, things improved somewhat. We were moved out of our dormitory-like residence into a proper house near the edge of the forest. It was nothing fancy. We had to draw water from a well that was even more primitive than the one in Biala Podlaska. I would lower a bucket—with a heavy piece of metal on the bottom so that it wouldn't float on the water's surface—and then bring it up by turning an ancient wooden crank.

Slowly, throughout that spring, we felt a bit of stability returning to our lives. Sol and I were assigned work in a large wood-processing factory specializing in parquet furniture, flooring, and wall coverings. My brother was an experienced cabinetmaker, but for me, not yet seventeen, this was a good introduction to precision woodworking. The factory, owned by a Belgian company before the war, was now, like almost every other business, operated by the Soviet state. But its sophisticated machinery still turned out finely

My mother and sister in Manievich in the spring of 1941

crafted products. Unusual woods, with striking natural colors such as black or red, were dried in a series of kilns for a week, masterfully cut, lacquered, and then assembled as mosaics. The finished products, almost as intricate as needlework tapestries, decorated homes or public buildings. Although I twice cut my thumb badly on a high-powered saw, I took pride in my work in the parquet factory. And I was able to bring home, under my winter coat, pieces of wood that we sorely needed for cooking and heating.

In April 1941, we were still anxious about our future but thankful to be sitting down together for the Passover Seder. Since we didn't feel at home in Manievich, our only thought was for a swift end to the war so that we could either return to Biala Podlaska or possibly immigrate to Palestine. But how long would that take? We had a small radio in the house and heard the news of Hitler's advances. We knew, too, by word of mouth, that Jews had been forced into ghettos all across German-occupied Poland. When, we wondered, would America enter the war and vanquish the Germans as it had done in World War I?

Our hope that Manievich would be a safe haven was extinguished on June 22, 1941. That day Germany launched a surprise attack against the Soviet Union, the country with which it had signed a nonaggression pact less than two years earlier. The invasion force of three million soldiers, along a fifteen-hundred-mile front, was the largest in world history.

From our beds throughout the early morning hours we heard the constant roar of low-flying heavy bombers. We were sure they had to be German and war had begun. This time no bombs fell on our town as they had on Biala Podlaska at the onset of hostilities. On the contrary, a deathly silence engulfed Manievich. People yearned for news but were at the mercy of Soviet broadcasts, which were muted and evasive. My brothers and I learned from a few railroad workers on their way home from the station that war between the two colossal powers had indeed broken out.

This was a far worse situation for us than in 1939. Then a friendly Soviet military had arranged for our evacuation. Now the Red Army itself was in chaos. It fought the Germans in some places, but the sudden assault had caught the high command in Moscow without a battle plan much less a thought about the civilians. Within three days, German motorized divisions were halfway across Volhynia. In less than a week, major towns and cities to the *east* of us, such as Rovno, fell to the invaders. We knew our turn was not far away.

The Jewish population of Manievich plunged into panic. As German bombs began to fall in the outskirts of town and Soviet troops retreated in disarray, we once again faced a life and death decision. Should we stay in Manievich? We had few illusions about the Nazis, even without knowing everything they were capable of since the Soviet news media had been silent about the terrible crimes committed by the country that had been its virtual ally. But from other refugees we had learned of the mutilation of Polish Jewry during the past two years and even heard rumors of fresh atrocities the Germans were committing as they overran Volhynia.

Yet to leave Manievich was equally terrifying. Should we wander the back roads without any destination? It was said that German planes had strafed columns of refugees fleeing by foot. Should we throw ourselves on the mercy of the Ukrainians? They saw Hitler as their deliverer from Stalinism and hoped by backing the Nazis their reward would be statehood. Ukrainian peasants were rumored to be erecting wooden crosses on the highways, with inscriptions welcoming German troops.

Above all, how could we break up our family when we had

already been through so much together? It was clear that some of us had no chance in trying to get away and would have to stay behind. My mother had been quite ill in Manievich and was bed-ridden at the time. Tateh, in his mid-fifties, was unsuited for a rough, dangerous journey into the unknown. And we were afraid that Moishe, despite his heroic exploits as a smuggler, was too young. The obstacles faced by us were faced by many. Indeed, I was not surprised to learn later that fewer than one out of twenty Volhynian Jews fled during the summer of 1941.

But Stalin's radio address to the nation on July 3, which we heard on a loudspeaker in front of a public building, changed our thinking. We and our neighbors had heard him many times before, always preceded by an announcer's introduction, delivered with the utmost gravity: *"Nemanyev, nemanyev! Gavarit Moscva."* (Attention, attention! Moscow speaking.) Although we never admired Stalin, we hoped for some guidance or assurance as he spoke for the first time since the invasion had begun almost two weeks earlier. Yet the "military genius," as he later called himself, simply urged us to allow nothing to fall into enemy hands. All supplies and equipment were to be shipped east. He didn't utter a word about civilians.

For my father, this was the final confirmation that we were now fully exposed to the Nazi beast. Within minutes he made the decision that was probably the most painful of his entire life: Simcha, Sol, and I would try to flee; he, my mother, and Moishe would stay, along with Sima, who would help care for Mameh and manage the household.

Tateh knew of a train—the last train east—that was due to leave Manievich in an hour. He hurried with his three oldest sons to the station before we could even pack one bag.

Even before we arrived we could make out a huge crowd of

people being held back by the local police. As we walked closer, we saw the train, on track number two, already overflowing with soldiers and civilians. It was a military transport carrying remnants of the defeated Red Army. But refugees, from our town and stops along the way, were holding onto every handle in the doorways and even sitting or lying on the roof.

We devised a plan to get aboard. To avoid the cops we would approach the tracks from the other side of the station, stay out of sight by creeping behind a low partition, and wedge ourselves into one of the cars. But there were too many police, too many people, and we hesitated. We told ourselves it was impossible to board the train and headed home, disappointed. At the same time we were relieved that our family was still together.

If we could have easily gotten on the train, we would have done so. This is what Tateh, and my mother too, I am sure, wanted for us. But while there was something pushing us forward there was also something holding us back. We were of two minds about breaking up the family and the difficulty getting aboard tipped the scales toward staying.

We never knew if that train ever made it out of the province. The railway line, which went as far as Kiev, was of major military significance and the heavy German bombardment likely destroyed the tracks to the east. Still, that train had offered the three of us—young, strong, and resourceful—a chance for survival. Even today I regret that we hadn't at least tried to get aboard.

The next few days were strangely quiet in Manievich as the last Soviet soldiers retreated, or, in many instances, went into hiding. And then, without warning on Friday evening July 6, our family was terrorized—by the Ukrainians. They had been kept at bay by the Soviets, but now, in the interval before the Germans arrived, they filled the power vacuum created by the Red Army's collapse.

In almost every town and village in the province they rose up and viciously attacked the Jews. There was no one to stop them.

With my father still at services, and Simcha and Sima away, six Ukrainian thugs armed with axes, knives, and clubs broke into our house and began tearing everything apart. Cursing at us, they turned mattresses over and cut them open looking for hidden valuables. They rifled through our drawers and threw the contents on the floor. They smashed the few pieces of furniture we had and knocked over everything on the shelves. Then they went to the kitchen where our modest Shabbes meal was sitting on the stove. They took the warm food out of the pots and pans and threw it at us as we shook with fright in a corner. Finally they carried off the utensils along with the rest of our cookware, some bedding and clothing, and most of our work tools. They also stole our radio.

We were appalled by this violation, this degradation. When Tateh, and later Simcha and Sima returned, we all worked glumly through the night to clean up the mess. It was like the house had been hit by a hurricane. Yet, we felt fortunate that we were the victims of nothing worse. From the way they acted, I feared those animals could have raped my mother or my sister had she been there, or simply killed us all.

The pogrom in Manievich raged for three days and nights. Gangs of Ukrainians pillaged almost every Jewish home, and we heard of instances of rape and murder along with the looting. By mid-July they had killed many hundreds of Jews across the province. I know that this savagery was to some extent triggered by a short-term cause: the eleventh-hour execution of some Ukrainian nationalists by members of the NKVD, the Soviet secret police. But there was a fury, a jealousy in their eyes that went much deeper than that.

In some Volhynian towns, the Jewish communities were so

shaken by this explosion of Ukrainian wrath that they actually asked the newly arrived German troops to control the violence. This, of course, was futile. Not only did the Nazis encourage some of these pogroms, but they invaded the Soviet Union with their own plan for dealing with the Jews—genocide.

FOUR

Purely by Chance

FOR MANY MONTHS before they began operating gas chambers in death camps like Auschwitz, the Germans sought to solve the "Jewish Problem" in the USSR through mass shootings. These were carried out by *Einsatzgruppen* (auxiliary units) of the SS that followed close on the heels of the regular German army. Four Einsatzgruppen operated in Soviet territory, and each was further divided into smaller "commando" units, usually supplemented by members of German police battalions. With the indispensable help of the native population—Lithuanians, Latvians and, in our region, enthusiastic Ukrainians—the invaders found Jews, herded them at gunpoint to fields or ravines outside of town, and shot them in huge pits. All four Einsatzgruppen combined numbered fewer than three thousand men, and they covered the vast expanse between Leningrad in the north and the Crimean Peninsula in the south, an area twice the size of Texas. But because of their close partnership with the locals they were able to murder a million Jews in a year and a half.

Without a fight our town fell to the German army at the end of the second week of July and we all braced ourselves for what would come next. Sol and I continued to work in the parquet factory; it would be a vital resource for us until the very end. Although the Nazis quickly seized it and shipped its products back to Germany, they did not have enough manpower to watch our every move. They left the day-to-day management of the plant in the hands of the Ukrainians. Employing more than a hundred people, the factory was a place to barter household goods, obtain a bit of food, and most important of all, exchange information.

In the short time they gave us for lunch, we heard horrifying stories of massacres in nearby towns from young Jews who had been able to get away. A few claimed to be eyewitnesses to the carnage. In most localities, we were told, it was the adult men whom the Einsatzgruppen had killed. In some cases, it was the leaders: rabbis, businessmen, and Jewish communal officials. Dozens, hundreds, even thousands of Jews at a time were said to have been murdered. Our desperation reached a new level.

Meanwhile, the occupiers imposed a ban on all travel and a stringent curfew. And quickly they ordered that we wear the Jewish star. At first it was to be displayed on an armband but within a matter of weeks they decreed two Jewish stars, sewn onto our jackets, both front and back. It was like walking around with two targets on your body. The penalty for being caught outside without the stars was a severe beating, no questions asked. They also decreed that a Jew had to doff his cap as a show of respect to a German, or even to a Ukrainian in a high position. We were prohibited from using the sidewalk if a German approached, though this directive meant little because there were few sidewalks in Manievich.

These edicts made us feel like we were in a big prison but the Germans weren't that visible in town. Except for an occasional motorcycle with a sidecar, we really didn't see much of them. The great help they received from the Ukrainians allowed them to control the entire province with fewer than a thousand men. They had no more than a few dozen soldiers in Manievich.

This thin German presence fed our illusions, as did the desire to avoid the pain of truly facing up to our situation. As the summer went on there was a lot of wishful thinking. Yes, we heard in July that in the city of Rovno several hundred Jews had been shot to death by the Einsatzgruppen, and in August, in Kamen-Kashirski, only thirty miles from us, a bloodbath had taken place. But we told ourselves it didn't mean that it would happen in Manievich. I don't know how firmly we believed it, but we actually said to one another that there might have been a *reason* why these mass killings had occurred elsewhere. The Jewish community of Rovno was much larger than ours, we argued, so how could anyone compare the two? Kamen-Kashirski was smaller, but wasn't it harboring Soviet agents and saboteurs?

In any case there didn't seem to be any real options. By then there was no doubt that we were surrounded both by German and Ukrainian murderers. This was not like France or Italy where you could knock on the door of a farmhouse or church and hope to be taken in. Our only chance was that the mobile killing units of the SS would somehow bypass Manievich. It was a slim possibility, but we clung to it. And with each passing day that awful summer the fact that we continued to be spared, that morning after morning we were still alive to see the sunrise, raised our hopes that the worst might still be avoided.

Our illusions ended on Friday, August 26. Documents published after the war revealed that we were the last of thirty-seven Volhynian communities hit by the Einsatzgruppen in the first phase of their plan to exterminate Soviet Jewry.

Sol and I had not gone to the parquet factory that day. Since midweek we had been on special assignment building furniture for a Ukrainian police officer in his house on a tiny farm at the edge of town. Near the end of the day he returned and commented, in a nonchalant but convincing way, that German commandos had come to Manievich, taken a lot of Jewish men and boys to a nearby village, and executed them. Stunned, we glanced at each other and just as casually asked permission to return home.

We ran back without speaking and found only our mother and sister. They were in a frenzied state but clearly told us what had happened: by late morning it had become apparent that a roundup of males was under way. Tateh, Simcha, and Moishe hid in an outhouse in the orchard about a hundred yards behind our house. Completely obscured from the street by fruit trees, it was a good hiding place even if it was cramped, hot, and foul smelling. Late in the afternoon, as the commotion of the "Jew hunt" quieted down, they emerged and dashed into our home. Too soon, it turned out. They were seen by the next-door neighbor, a middle-aged Ukrainian man, who left and came back fifteen minutes later with a detachment of police that seized the three of them, and led them away.

Mameh was so distraught she tore out clumps of her hair. And yet she clung to the hope they might still be alive, in fact pressed her face to the window believing they might come back at any minute. We had heard that the roundups, especially if they only went after the men, were sometimes for the purpose of forced labor, not for execution. This was also the pretext given by the Nazis themselves. Sol, Sima, and I—her surviving three children—tried to comfort her. He and I had no doubt that our oldest and youngest brother and our father had been murdered during the last few hours. We later told Sima what we had heard from the Ukrainian police officer, but we never told our mother.

Standing in that grief-stricken house I was overcome by the loss of three people I loved deeply and filled with rage at the way their lives were taken. At the same time it was bewildering that Sol and I were spared. I doubted if there was any meaning to human existence.

From conversations with people during the next weeks and months, and accounts of eyewitnesses published after the war, I learned how Tateh, Simcha, and Moishe were killed. After they were betrayed by our neighbor, Ukrainian police broke into our house and made them march to the center of town. There, with some other Jews who had been captured in this last sweep of the day, they were pushed into an open truck that resembled a cage with metal bands on its top and sides. Standing up, they were driven about four miles into the countryside to the outskirts of a small village, Gereyvara. There they were ordered out of the vehicle and made to walk through a grove of tall pines into an open clearing. It was called Ferdishe Mogiles, or Horses' Graves, because for many years horse carcasses were buried there.

Now it had become a killing field for human beings. What my father and brothers saw were three long ditches, each piled to the top with dead, naked bodies. Blood, excrement, and pieces of human flesh and organs were bubbling in those rivers of hell.

They were forced by the Ukrainian guards to undress completely and in the last minutes of their lives were cursed and beaten. My father and brothers were thrown into one of the pits, on top of four or five layers of corpses. Then an SS man, one of several who had been executing people with his submachine gun for more than an hour, shot them to death. Standing near the ditch, he aimed at the back of their heads, but there is no telling where the bullets entered their bodies.

Then it was over. Tateh, Simcha, and Moishe were among the

very last of three hundred and seventy Jewish males of Manievich to be slaughtered that day. Peasants who had dug the ditches early in the morning now covered them with earth. The Ukrainian guards returned to Manievich that evening for a festive meal. Many of them had volunteered for the day's work of finding and capturing Jews, leading them to their deaths, and preventing escapes. They did everything but pull the trigger. The Germans paid them with all the vodka they could carry.

The SS machine gunners drank, too, in some cases even while they carried out the mass murder. Their mission accomplished, the men of *Sonderkommando* 4a of Einsatzgruppe C packed up and left the area. In ten weeks they had put to death more than fifteen thousand Jews in Volhynia. After a month of perpetrating other atrocities, this unit was ordered two hundred and fifty miles to the east, where it exterminated thirty-three thousand Jewish residents of Kiev in a ravine called Babi Yar.

A thousand times I've endured the pain of turning this over in my mind trying to imagine what my father and brothers were thinking at the end. Tateh probably rued his sons' aborted attempt to flee by train less than two months earlier. Simcha, a tough and aggressive young man, must have been trying to figure out a way to escape the killers' clutches. Had he been taken earlier in the day, among a larger group of Jews, maybe he could have broken free. But by late afternoon he was one of a small remnant that was guarded by many Ukrainians. And hiding all day in the outhouse, without food or water, might have weakened him physically. Moishe was a child of eleven. He must have looked to his father and biggest brother to protect him.

There is little doubt that if Sol and I had not been working in the home of the Ukrainian police officer we, too, would have been shot in that bloody pit. We would easily have been picked up in the parquet factory, a main target of the raid that day.

For many years I believed that the police officer who came home and told us of the executions was a participant, not a mere witness. Such a high percentage of Ukrainian police were involved in these killings—ten for every German—it was hard to believe he wasn't in on it. But then, why didn't he send the police to capture us during the day? He knew exactly where we were and we would have been taken by surprise. Even if he didn't want it known that Jews were working for him in his house, he could have gotten us to go out on some errand and then had us arrested. As for the furniture we were making for him, the job was nearly done by Friday. And if furniture was on his mind, everyone knew it could easily be plundered from Jewish homes, all the more so after a massacre.

The Ukrainian police knew of this SS *Aktion* days in advance because they were the ones who prepared lists with the names and addresses of Jewish families, recruited the volunteers, and picked the execution site. Could this police officer have pulled us out of the parquet factory to save our lives? Did he have us work in his home where he knew that no one would think of looking for Jews? And if, indeed, he spared us in this way, why? We barely knew him; he only hired us after a brief inquiry for carpenters he had made at the factory a week before.

Even among the Ukrainians there was a handful of good people who helped Jews. Maybe he was one of them. It is even possible that he played a role *both* in killing three members of my family *and*, for some reason, in saving my life and Sol's. Or, that he did neither. However it happened, I felt that I was left alive purely by chance.

Sol and I were now among the few Jewish men remaining in Manievich. After a couple of days we went back to work in the parquet factory. Every evening we returned to a house of unimaginably low spirits. I don't think my mother ever stopped crying after August 26. She continued to light candles every Shabbes, but it was more to mark that horrendous Friday evening than to usher in a day of rest. There was no funeral for my father and brothers, no *shiva*, and no *kaddish*. But we were a family in deep mourning nonetheless.

In the fall the Germans further tightened their grip on our decimated Jewish community. As elsewhere in Eastern Europe they formed a *Judenrat,* or Jewish Council, in Manievich to carry out their directives. It included about a half dozen Jewish leaders who had survived the bloodshed and was headed by a lawyer named Frucht, a refugee from central Poland like us, who was probably chosen for his good knowledge of German. The Judenrat oversaw the food rationing, handed out work assignments, and controlled housing and health care. In the larger population centers of Volhynia, cities such as Rovno and Kovel, the Judenrat had even greater powers, including the task of confiscating furs and jewels from Jews and turning them over to the Germans. Because our little town was relatively poor, however, there were few such levies.

The Judenrat was also in charge of a small force of Jewish policemen armed with rubber clubs. They came from the lowest level of society and frequently were ex-convicts. Like the Judenrat, the Jewish police were usually corrupt. Drunk with power, a Jewish cop could think he was "Moishe Groys," a big shot. And he could be very cruel.

One day, while Sol was away, a big, brutish Jewish policeman barged into our house and went after Sima. She had broken one of the rules—I can't recall which one—and he proceeded to beat her right in front of my mother and me. He survived Manievich and later ended up in the same partisan unit as I did. Several times I was ready to kill him—I actually had him in my line of fire—but I couldn't bring myself to pull the trigger.

To this day I feel a great deal of anger toward the leaders of the Judenrat also. I realize they were in an impossible situation and they had to do the bidding of the Germans. But I cannot forgive them for not doing *other* things at the same time, for failing to coordinate any real response to the horror we were living through. They could have tried to obtain arms; they could have helped organize escapes. Instead, they instructed the Jewish police to prevent anyone from leaving. At the very least they could have funneled some accurate information our way about resistance efforts being undertaken by others. Because they hoped to save their own lives, the only strategy they adopted was to do nothing on our behalf and to give in to every German demand. Indeed, the very existence of this Jewish "government" played into the Nazis' hands because it created an illusion of "business as usual," making it easier for us to remain in a state of denial and inaction. We would have actually fared better without any intermediary between the occupiers and us.

Early in 1942, the Judenrat decreed that all Jews would be concentrated in two ghettos, one near the center of town and the other about a mile away across the railroad tracks. These differed from the infamous Warsaw and Lodz ghettos that went up earlier in that there were no barriers separating us from the outside. But except for work we were not allowed to leave. And because of the curfew we could not even go out of our houses after 6 P.M. Our ghetto, in the middle of Manievich, held about three hundred Jews on a few blocks along one muddy street, Budgasse. Sol and I probably received favorable treatment because of the jobs we held in the parquet factory since we were among the few not forced to share our dilapidated two-room home with other families. There was even a barn in the back of the house they assigned us, empty of animals but still filled with hay.

Food became an even greater problem once we were confined to the ghetto. It was almost impossible to get meat. We had stockpiled dried fruits and vegetables in the cellar of our former house but were given such a short time to vacate—a few hours—that we had to leave most of it behind. Our ration cards entitled us to meager amounts of bread, potatoes, and kasha (half of what the Ukrainians received), and Sol and I were provided a little bread for lunch in the factory. The only way we survived was to buy food, or barter for it, on the black market.

About a month after we moved into the ghetto my sister vanished. Sima left the house one day, and we never saw her again. It is unlikely that she tried to escape Manievich because so few thought about that in the spring of 1942. And even if she had, she would have shared her plans with Sol and me. Sima would have said goodbye to her mother, to whom she had been deeply devoted, and to her brothers. Sol and I frantically searched Budgasse but we couldn't find a trace of her. I felt completely powerless. My only guess is that she left the ghetto—an extremely dangerous act at that time—with the intention of buying something or visiting someone, and that she was attacked by Germans or Ukrainians and killed. She was just short of her thirtieth birthday.

That left only three of us. My mother had little will to go on living. All that she wanted now was for Sol and me to survive. Passover of 1942 came and went. We had no Seder and did not mark the "time of our freedom" in any way.

By summer the talk in the parquet factory grew even more ominous. Some new workers arrived, Jews from surrounding villages who had been forced into our ghetto. Nearly all of us had lost loved ones in the butchery of the year before and were embittered beyond description. But now the rumors were of something worse: a Nazi plot to murder *all* the Jews, not "merely" most of the men. This is why we were concentrated in the ghettos, said some of the newcomers—to make it easier for them to kill us all. In August one of them said that the fifteen thousand Jews of Kovel had been liquidated, a claim that was impossible to verify then but later turned out to be true.

For the first time, a plan of action emerged: escape into the woods. This had not been considered feasible before. We were close to the forest, but it was a vast timberland, dotted with only a few small farms and tiny villages, and we had neither a guide, nor a map. How would we find food? How would we keep from freezing to death in the severe winter of this region? How would we defend ourselves against wild animals? And even if, by some miracle, we kept ourselves alive in the wilderness, wouldn't the Germans, with the aid of the local population, just hunt us down with dogs?

But we had heard vague reports of groups operating in the woods, people opposed to the Nazis. Some spoke of former Red Army men who had broken out of POW camps or had been in hiding since their army's collapse. Others told of anti-fascist cadres of Poles and even Ukrainians. Something was out there.

Yet Sol and I hesitated. I found out later that by the end of August there *were* a handful of young Jews, in Manievich and the surrounding villages, communicating with such groups. They fled the ghetto with a couple of guns and, with the aid of a sympathetic Polish forester, were able to join the partisans.

My brother and I, however, knew nothing of this. Like most Jews in our town we had no firm knowledge of any specific bands in the forest, much less an idea of where they were. To us, it was talk, nothing more. And in the same discussions people said how futile it would be to run into the woods. The fatalism among both religious and non-religious Jews had only deepened by that time. Most of those conversations ended with someone saying, "It really doesn't matter if you go into the forest or you don't. Because what's the difference if you die there or you die here?"

But Sol and I wanted to live. As the summer wore on, I began to believe another rumor going around the factory: The Germans were about to consolidate the two ghettos into one, the ghetto south of the train station. It would be sealed tight, and then annihilated. My instincts told me that moving to the other ghetto meant death, that there couldn't be any other reason why they'd squeeze all of us into one place. I convinced Sol of this. Whatever happens, he agreed with me, we would not move to that other ghetto; to go there would be suicide.

Friday, September 3, 1942. Somehow, the way an animal senses danger, I had a sickening feeling that this could be the day. We had been told the day before not to report for work in the parquet factory, only adding to our fears. The talk on the street was that the other ghetto was already being enclosed.

In the late morning I came across a few family pictures lying on the kitchen table. Without thinking, without looking through them carefully, I put them in my pocket.

The killers came at the end of the day. I happened to be in the backyard and ran to a hiding place in the barn. I could hear the bedlam of the roundup outside. At dusk, a Ukrainian guard climbed up to the loft where I lay buried in a mound of hay, checked the area, and missed me. I remained motionless and an hour later was startled by another Jewish runaway, at the other end of the hayloft, who had concealed himself even before I had. Shleimeh, quite a few years older than I, had recently been trans-

ferred to the ghetto from a nearby village and was a stranger. We
waited until the middle of the night and then crawled to the safety
of the forest.

The only two people I loved in the world were not so fortunate.
Many months later I learned that Sol and Mameh were brutally
forced into a truck and transported to the enclosed ghetto. Late
that night, along with Simcha's former girlfriend and her brother,
Sol tried to escape by scaling a wooden fence and making a run
for it. The girl and her brother made it to freedom, but they told
me that Sol was shot dead in the attempt. In a way, he had saved
my life. It was probably due to his reputation as a skilled crafts-
man that we were both selected to make furniture in a remote
farmhouse during the bloody sweep of August 1941.

And now, a year later, I could do nothing to save him.

On Saturday, the ghetto was liquidated. Although I don't know
the exact details, I can't imagine how my mother could have avoided the fate of almost all of the other Jews remaining in Manievich.
Even though death camps such as Sobibor and Belzec were in
operation and less than a day's train ride away, the Germans evidently had no concerns about executing the Volhynian Jews in full
view of the local population. Once again they had peasants dig the
death pits, this time fairly close to town. And now they murdered
every Jew—man, woman, and child, including the sick and the
elderly—that they and their Ukrainian collaborators could find.

Daybreak after the roundup found Shleimeh and me deep in the
forest, dazed and totally disoriented. We were also very hungry. Fortunately it was late summer and there were blackberries to be picked,
even some cabbage and potatoes. Creeks ran with fresh water.

While I satisfied my body's hunger and thirst for the time
being, my spirit was shattered. Although I was only eighteen, I

knew that if I survived I would never be whole again. The year before we had all sat around the dinner table, a family of seven. Now, in all likelihood, I was the only one of the Epelbaum family still alive.

It was such a shock that I was numb during those first few days in the woods. I wouldn't even allow myself to think too long about what had just taken place.

I had to focus on what was going to happen to me and my fellow fugitive. The forest was our friend *now*, but in a matter of a few short weeks the weather would change and it would get cold. Food would become scarce. The trees would lose their leaves and we would become more visible from the roads and the air. After the first snowfall, if we survived until then, our footprints would give us away.

At mid-morning we came across a narrow dirt road with ruts on either side from wagon wheels. It seemed to veer away from Manievich, heading north and deeper into the woods. Instead of walking along this road we remained about fifty yards from it, hidden by the trees, yet able to see who might be coming. Neither did we venture too far in one direction or another since we didn't know where that artery led; after a few miles we would retrace our steps. So it wasn't long before we came to learn the terrain of one small part of the forest fairly well.

But mostly we kept our eyes on that road. It was the only thing that could bring us help. We let peasants in their horse-drawn carts drive by. Soon we encountered another escaped Jew, and then two more. Within a few days we had grown into a group of eight or nine Jewish men who had escaped into the forest the evening of the roundup. All were as unprepared as I was.

Yet I felt a little better being with more people, hearing their stories and telling mine. Now we had more decision-makers and could organize ourselves into small teams. Two or three of us would approach a peasant's house at night and try to steal any food left outside. A few others would go off in another direction and scout the terrain. Someone else would remain to watch the traffic on the wagon road. We mostly ate potatoes quickly baked over a fire. We would warm them further in the hot ashes and eat them in their crisp skins. At night we slept on beds of leaves.

But after a few weeks it was clear time was running out. If there was an organized resistance group in this forest with food and clothing, with horses, guns, and a radio, we had to make contact with them soon.

One day in late September it seemed that our hope was answered. We spotted three armed men on horseback confidently riding down the wagon road. It was the head of a partisan unit and two of his aides.

We all crowded around the leader, a Polish communist in his thirties who went by the name of Maks. He only revealed a few details about himself, but later I pieced together his story. Like me, he came from the province of Lublin and fled into the Soviet zone of occupation when the Germans invaded Poland in 1939. After the Nazi onslaught during the summer of 1941, he served as a spy for Moscow and ran an underground press in Manievich that printed dissident leaflets. The Ukrainian police soon arrested and jailed him. But on the way to Gestapo headquarters in Kovel, he escaped into the woods and from then on was constantly on the run, harbored by a series of sympathetic peasants. In memoirs published after the war under his real name, Jozef Sobiesiak, he wrote that during the harsh winter of 1941–42 he felt like the only anti-Nazi in the entire forest.

Since the spring, he had been organizing a partisan force whose nucleus included a few Poles and a number of former Soviet soldiers who were still in the area. And he was joined by nine anti-fascist Ukrainians led by the hot-tempered communist Mikola Konishchuk, whose *nom de guerre* was Kruk. Although they would soon split off from Maks, and form their own group, the two units would remain in close contact and work in tandem.

Maks, who we later learned had an informer in the Manievich police station, knew of most Nazi intentions in advance. He had been aware of the plan to liquidate the ghetto and, several days before it happened, tried to enter the town and organize a mass escape. Unfortunately, he had to abort the mission. Now that the worst had happened, he was trying to assess the usefulness to his outfit of the hundred or so surviving Jews roaming the forest in small, isolated groups. He sized us up in a friendly way. We could tell he was a Pole with fewer anti-Semitic prejudices than most and also saw that he was dedicated to fighting Hitler. So we trusted him almost immediately.

But Maks would not accept us. The reason was simple. We didn't have one gun among us. Weapons were all that mattered at this stage. Without them we would be worse than useless; we would be a burden. Naturally, the rejection was devastating. But before he and his comrades rode off, Maks left the door open. He gave us the feeling that he was thinking things over and that he'd likely return.

What if he didn't? Lacking any heavy clothing, we contemplated the cold weather that was almost upon us. The previous winter had been brutal even by the standards of this frigid area. In the ghetto, with heating fuel hard to come by, some Jews almost froze to death inside their rickety houses. What would we do now, exposed without any shelter at all?

Maybe we could keep warm with a fire during the day, we told ourselves, and somehow vent the smoke so that it wouldn't give away our position. Maybe we could hide in barns at night. Maybe, even unarmed, we could overwhelm a peasant and take his gun. Then with one gun we could get food, horses, and perhaps more weapons. But as we talked, our plans sounded so improbable. Although no one ever said it out loud, we all knew that Maks was our only salvation.

He did return about two weeks after the first meeting. We numbered about two dozen by then, including some women. All of us were growing desperate in the chilly weather of early October. But this time Maks took us in, all of us. His men had stolen some extra guns from a remote farmhouse. We would go with him to his camp and some of us would be armed right away.

Maks himself put a sawed-off shotgun into my hands. I had never fired a gun before. In fact, I had never even held one. It wasn't a Jewish thing to do. But I learned fast.

FIVE

In the Partisans

MAKS AND HIS MEN led us deeper into the forest. Walking behind them, I saw the landscape begin to change. About ten or twelve miles north of Manievich, the dense woods gave way to marshland and swamps. No motorized vehicles could come after us here. Of course this spongy terrain would freeze in the winter, and we would lose the protection it afforded us. But for now it was impassable to a modern army and treacherous for any man or beast that didn't know the way. One false step and you'd fall into the bog up to your waist.

On a stretch of higher, drier ground—almost an island in the wetlands—sat the partisan camp. I stared in wonderment as a virtual "forest republic" came into view, living proof that the Nazis had not triumphed completely. Dozens of armed young men confidently moved about, and there was a much larger group of noncombatants, almost all of them Jews—about a hundred and fifty men, women, old people, and even small children. On the outer clothing of some of the civilians you could see where they had recently removed the Jewish stars they had been forced to wear in the Volhynian ghettos during more than a year of Nazi rule.

This was the core of a group that would grow to over five hundred within the next few months, a civilian community that Maks and his fighters fed, clothed, and protected until the liberation in 1944. Only a minority of partisan brigades maintained non-combatants and even then it would usually be just a handful of people needed for essential jobs. "He who does not fight, does not eat" was the policy of most commanders because it was so hard to find food in the countryside. No less critical was the question of mobility. How could a partisan band move on short notice if it was also responsible for a large contingent of refugees?

But Maks, perhaps influenced by the Jewish woman with whom he lived while commanding the partisans (and whom he would marry after the war), felt a strong obligation to every victim of Nazism, every fugitive in the forest, whether the person could carry a gun or not. I wasn't fully aware of it at the time, but he had to fight hard to convince his lieutenants—and later his superiors—that he was on the right course. With the struggle for survival on everyone's mind in the fall of 1942, it would have been the easiest thing for him to agree that harboring non-combatants was a luxury we couldn't afford. But Maks prevailed, and ours was by far the largest civilian camp in the province and among the biggest in all of Eastern Europe.

We kept them alive and in return the civilians helped us fighters in countless ways. They prepared our food, washed and mended our clothes, and repaired our equipment. They gathered berries, mushrooms, and herbs from the forest floor. And they raised our spirits with their encouragement and gratitude. As time went on, life for the civilians became more stable and secure. Some of them even observed the Jewish holidays and in 1943 they had a Passover

Seder. Disease and cold weather naturally took their toll, but about two thirds of the refugees we sheltered survived the war.

All of the credit goes to Maks. But this righteous gentile who saved my life and hundreds of others also had his dark side. Like a warlord in the wilderness, he ruled the camp with a quick temper and an iron hand. He personally meted out punishment for any infraction of the rules. For a serious crime, the penalty could be severe. Although I did not witness it, several men in the brigade claimed that on a whim he shot to death a well-liked Jewish partisan whom he wrongly suspected of being a traitor. Whether or not this story is true, the fact remains that Maks, a large man who wore a revolver on his hip and carried a sixty-round submachine gun on his shoulder, intimidated us all.

He also had a serious drinking problem. He consumed vast quantities of *samagon*, strong vodka that the peasants distilled in their homes and that he made even more potent by adding honey. I sometimes saw him staggering in front of his quarters before noon. He was a womanizer, too. Despite the presence of his common-law wife in the camp, he had numerous affairs. And he also saw to it that he and his friends, both men and women, had far better living accommodations than the rest of us.

But for all of that he was among the best of the partisan commanders. Most others were even more selfish and tyrannical, and many were ardent anti-Semites. At first our group had two leaders, Maks and Kruk, the latter a crude and illiterate peasant who had served as a village chief during the Soviet occupation a few years earlier. Kruk seemed always on the verge of erupting into a fit of anger that could turn deadly. His own men often distrusted him. Early on we split into separate units and I was selected by Maks to stay with him. I probably would have survived had I gone with Kruk—and as it turned out he had a higher proportion of Jews than Maks did—but I never would have admired him as much as I did Maks.

Yes, Maks had some glaring personal failings. But I was in awe of his strength as a leader: the courage and good judgment he showed in moments of the greatest danger; his "hands-on" style of management; and, of course, the responsibility he assumed for even the most vulnerable civilians. He had not gone to college to learn his job, nor did he have any formal credentials for it. He took on his role without being elected or appointed by anybody and simply ruled by the force of his personality. In making the major decisions he sometimes consulted others, but we had nothing approaching a democracy and there was never any doubt who was in charge. For that time and in that place, I cannot imagine any other social arrangement that would have made more sense.

When I first arrived in October 1942, the camp was in the process of being built. I joined the construction crew working on the semi-underground bunkers that typically housed partisans throughout Eastern Europe. Prior to their completion, we slept out in the open. But with winter rapidly approaching, we needed enclosed quarters that would also be largely concealed. The solution, the *ziemlanka* (a derivative of the Russian word for soil) was ingenious in its simplicity.

Selecting the highest mound we could, in order to avoid the groundwater so prevalent in this area, we would dig down about three and a half feet. Then, inside the earthen pit, we'd build something like a log cabin. The plentiful birch wood was the easiest to work with; tall, thin, and supple, the tree trunks were roughly the same diameter from top to bottom. We carefully notched the ends to form the corners of the enclosure and used dried moss as a sealant between logs. Wary of water leaks, we sometimes lined the walls with cowhides. The pitched roof of the ziemlanka, also made of slim logs, rose only three or four feet above the ground. To shed the rainwater, as well as offer a bit of camouflage and insulation, we covered it with hay, straw, and tree branches. From a distance you could barely make it out.

Before long we completed almost a dozen of these forest barracks, building them long and narrow. People slept close to one another for warmth, in two rows of about fifteen people each. The center aisle was not wide and usually contained a wood-burning heater, vented with a pipe fashioned from tin cans.

Cooking was done outside, in fifty-gallon barrels cut in half. They were hung by a heavy chain from a log crossbeam, high off the ground, attached to two sturdy poles. Later the women chiseled a stone slab with holes in it for several kettles. Underneath they ignited a large fire fed by wood and coal, which burned day and night.

In those huge, boiling pots we cooked mostly meat. Our main source of food was the surrounding villages and estates where there was abundant livestock raised by peasants. We would return at night from food-foraging expeditions with animals that we'd eat the next day. In addition to lamb, beef, or pork, we usually had potatoes. So our staple was meat soup, which we ate for breakfast, lunch, and dinner all year long.

We preferred taking pigs from the farms rather than cows or sheep, since the meat kept longer. We would shoot the swine in the barn—of course this was a different kind of butchering than I was used to—throw them on our wagons and take them back to camp. One part of the pig provided us with the food reserve essential for our survival in the winter. This was the three- or four-inch-thick slab of white fatback, essentially bacon, that we skinned, salted, and stored layer upon layer in barrels. It could be cooked or, if we were on the move, eaten raw. Best of all, it would last for months. Called *sala* by the Ukrainians, it was usually sliced with a knife despite its buttery texture and eaten with a quarter loaf of black bread.

This was anything but a balanced diet. In fact, once the freezing weather arrived, fruits and vegetables were so scarce that we had a problem with scurvy. To fight it, we were provided with a substance to rub on our gums.

An even more common health hazard was lice, which caused us endless torment. Because we each had only one set of clothes and boots, and, for security reasons, lived, worked, and slept in them in very tight quarters, the plague spread rapidly. No part of the body was immune. Even if you didn't have lice, the person next to you, constantly scratching, would keep you up all night.

We tried all sorts of remedies to rid ourselves of the tiny insects and their eggs. Some people boiled or froze their clothes, while others held their clothing about half an inch away from the fire hoping to kill the lice without singeing the fabric. Some tried ointments that gave off a bad smell. All I did was squeeze the nits between my thumb and forefinger. But nothing really worked. Even if I threw away an infested piece of clothing and got a new one, two weeks later the lice would reappear.

So I tried to replace my clothes often except for an outer garment I wore throughout nearly all of my service with the partisans and even for a long time after the liberation. It was the tightly knit, dark blue dress coat worn by Soviet naval officers, with a stiff collar an inch and a half high and a row of fancy buttons down the front. Brought into our camp by a former Red Army man who joined our group, it was a strange outfit for an eighteen-year-old who had been a factory worker and ghetto dweller just months before. The well-made coat not only bolstered my confidence, but its heavy underlayment also kept the wind and rain out. Many of the other partisans wore leather jackets, and some even had the same long cloth coats they brought from home. We had to follow many rules, but unlike the regular army, standards for clothing were not among them. Everyone was on his own.

We were also pretty much free to decide how we would spend the long evening hours. Of course, we all were assigned guard duty, usually two-hour shifts, a lonely task but one that had the highest priority. The rest of the time was spent inside the bunkers in order to stay warm. There we entertained ourselves with song and dance. About half of the partisans were Russians, and they tended to love music. Many of them had instruments, the accordion or more frequently the triangular, three-stringed balalaika that sounds like a mandolin. Most nights a handful of Russians would get up and begin playing and the rest of us would sing along. Sometimes there were ballads, like "Dark Night" with its sad refrain, "Nobody will ever know where you're buried when you get killed at the front." Other songs were more patriotic and upbeat, such as "Three Tankmen and Three Happy Fellows." Some tunes were raucous, to which they danced the classic *kazatzka*. There were storytelling sessions, too, a never-ending supply of jokes (including some of the coarsest imaginable), and always lots of vodka to go around.

There were a good many women among us, mostly civilians but also some fighters. And when we finally went to sleep it was not unusual for people to pair off and be intimate. But for us Jews it was not sex with wild abandon. All of the music and alcohol in the world could not lighten the burden of knowing that our families had recently been murdered. Nothing could ease the trauma of what we had just been through in the ghettos, and in our flights into the forest. So young Jews coupled with heavy, mournful feeling. More than the satisfaction of desire, sex was a source of comfort, a kind of balm.

It was also a currency to be traded for protection. The women in the camp, a high percentage of them Jewish, felt quite vulnerable among the hard-drinking Russians, Poles, and Ukrainians. However, if they took one of these fighters as a steady boyfriend, especially if he was physically strong, well armed, or in Maks' inner circle, they would be defended against all the others. I saw a number of instances in which refined, educated Jewish girls from middle-class families ended up not only with non-Jews but also with men who had been menial laborers before the war, the kind of people that outside the forest they would have had nothing to do with.

Myself, I did not have a girlfriend while in the partisans. For one thing everyone having lice wasn't very romantic. But the real reason was that the intensity of those days—the dangerous missions and the hurly-burly of camp life—absorbed every ounce of my energy. I did have my first sexual experience at this time. It was with a peasant girl in a barn on a farm where we went to seek food. But I knew I wasn't ready for a serious relationship with a woman in Maks' brigade.

Whether or not you had a mate, life in the forest was one of extreme hardship. Not only the Germans, but also the ferocious Ukrainian partisan bands were out to kill us. The cold weather was crushing and the supply of food was never secure. We suffered from mosquito-borne diseases in the summer, scurvy and pneumonia in the winter, and lice throughout the year. There were all sorts of personal conflicts among people from vastly different backgrounds who had been thrown together overnight. And the camp was run by a dictator, normally a benevolent despot, but in any case someone we all had to obey.

Not everyone was willing to endure these conditions. Some of those who threw in their lot with Maks complained loudly from the very beginning. It wasn't that different from the ancient Israelites who turned on Moses in the desert and said that things had been better in Egypt. And Maks had no manna from heaven to give these malcontents. Despite his strong attempt to dissuade them, some Jews actually returned to the ghetto in the fall of 1942 refusing to believe that the Germans had liquidated their communities. As soon as they walked out of the forest, of course, they were doomed.

In his memoirs, Maks wrote of a tragic defection that took place shortly before my arrival. The rabbi of a village not far from Manievich, hearing that the Germans had put up posters promising not to harm Jews who came out of hiding on their own, convinced about a hundred of his flock to go home with him. Every one of them, including the incredibly naïve rabbi, was murdered in short order.

Never once did it cross my mind to leave Maks. Even if I'd had a plan to survive in town, a safe hiding place, for example, I would not have taken that route. Although daily life was extremely rough as a partisan, I was a free man. Maks demanded unquestioning loyalty, and I, for one, willingly and gratefully gave it to him.

With so many people in camp, we were under great pressure to obtain large quantities of provisions and my first mission was a food-gathering expedition. Referring to a map, Maks ordered four of us to ride to a remote farmhouse he had selected. At gunpoint, if necessary, we were to carry off the peasant's animals, as well as any bread, beans, or canned food he might have. If he had a great deal on hand, we were told to load everything on his wagons and take them with his horses, too. Half a dozen groups of partisans

Maks (center) planning a mission

rode off on horseback in different directions for the same purpose each night.

It is hard to describe the euphoria I felt riding out of camp with my new comrades and that old sawed-off shotgun slung across my chest. Because ammunition was so precious, I was not given any training with the weapon. I was just expected to put the shells into the chamber, aim, and fire. Merely holding that gun and knowing that I could rip a person apart transformed me. For three years I had felt like a scared little boy—anybody could do anything to me and to my family. Now I was in the position of scaring others. I felt like a king, in a way, because when you visit a monarch you have to bow and take three steps back. I now realized that fear of the gun would have much the same effect on people.

That first assignment went well. The farmer and his wife, hostile to our cause, stood by in silence as we cleaned out their cupboards and rounded up their livestock. The Germans put up posters referring to us as "bandits" and this must have been how we appeared to many people.

Nonetheless, as time went on we found goodwill on the part of most of the local population. An increasing number of peasants, and sometimes entire villages, began to see the Nazi occupation for what it was and developed sympathy for the refugees we were feeding in the forest. Turning over food, clothing, or household goods became almost a form of taxation or charity. On our part, if a farmer were friendly we would take only a portion of what he had, always leaving him and his family more than enough produce and livestock to survive. On occasion, peasants even asked us what we needed and voluntarily helped us load it on our wagons. Going back to the same farmhouses again and again, we were even greeted by name. We felt that we had finally won some allies.

It was a different story when we went into the countryside searching for guns. Firearms were guarded like life itself and surrendered only as a last resort. But we desperately needed them. We knew that there were caches of arms hidden on farms throughout the area. Most peasants owned hunting rifles. Also, the collapse of the Polish army in 1939, as well as the rapid retreat of the Soviets two years later, resulted in many weapons being left behind.

In the course of one of our early expeditions we questioned a farmer who convinced us that a peasant in another village was hiding guns. He gave us directions to the man's house, and the following night a few of us rode out to see for ourselves. We delivered a clear ultimatum: We know you have guns and either you give them up or we kill you. He swore up and down that we were mistaken. We believed our source and threatened one last time to shoot him if he did not reveal the hiding place. But he continued his denial.

So we pushed him out of the house and into his barn where we held him down on the dirt floor. We grabbed a rope and tied it around his waist. Then we took a long, thick pole, put it between the rope and his abdomen, and started turning. It didn't take many revolutions of the pole for him to submit. We loosened the rope and allowed him to stand up. He motioned us to a spot outside the barn and proceeded to dig up four fine guns, not the old sawed-off kind I had, but rifles with full-length barrels. When we returned to camp, Maks let me keep one. It had a clip for ten rounds and would serve as my weapon until almost the end of my stay with the partisans.

Occasionally we were bold enough to raid village police stations for guns. Because we couldn't just barge in through the front door, we developed diversionary tactics. We would creep up with straw and other kindling and place it behind the building. Then we'd pour on gasoline, light it, and yell "Fire!" in Ukrainian. As the policemen ran out the front of the station, we'd be ready and mow them down. Even if a few got away, they usually left their weapons behind. We would rush in and take anything we needed.

The best-stocked arsenal in the area was the big police station in Manievich. Yet, during the entire course of the war we never attacked it. We heard they put up barriers of logs around the entire circumference as a precaution, but that is not what deterred us. We avoided it because of Maks' informer in the station house. The commander would do nothing that might disrupt the steady flow of intelligence from that critical listening post. In fact, he declared the whole town off-limits.

But the countryside was full of people who informed on *us* whenever they could. They were the greatest threat to our survival. Mostly Ukrainian fascists who were both peasants and part-time policemen, many of them had participated in the mass killings carried out by the Einsatzgruppen during the previous two summers. Now they betrayed Jews who were still hiding in farmhouses, and they reported on our activities to the Germans.

It wasn't long before Maks broadened our mission to deal with these collaborators. At night, a group of four or five us would arrive at the house of a perpetrator—an informer, a murderer, or someone who was both—and at first pretend we were just after his food. We would force him to load up his horse-drawn cart with provisions and then order him to come with us so that he could drive the empty wagon back home from our camp. But on the way we'd stop on a back road, order the man to get out, and execute him with a bullet to the head. It felt good to get back at these fiends who had the blood of our families on their hands. But it should also be said that our team showed them some mercy since we never killed their innocent wives or children.

Yet in late 1942, an act of betrayal was so heinous that Maks felt we had to make an example of the informer. He would not be sent to his grave with a single pistol shot. Rather, we would make him die a slow, terrible death. This was a peasant who was such a dedicated Nazi sympathizer, we learned from several farmers, that he had made the long trip from his village into town to tell the Germans of Jews being harbored by his next-door neighbor. He was then spotted returning with the SS and directing them to the hiding place, where they found the refugees and took them away along with the family that had sheltered them.

A few nights later, on Maks' orders, four of us abducted this informer and brought him with us into the forest. We stopped in a remote spot to cook a late supper. Although frightened, he was not altogether sure of our intentions and actually helped us get the fire going. When it was good and hot we let him in on the fact that we knew what he had done. Of course he denied it. But we had no doubt about his guilt; we had talked with eyewitnesses. We shot him several times, and, while he was still alive, threw him on the fire.

As I write this, I wonder if my grandchildren, born in America and Israel at the turn of the new century, may have difficulty understanding such an act of cold-blooded revenge when they are old enough to think about such horrific things. It was a human being, after all, whom we not only killed but also tortured. But in this time of bloodletting in Eastern Europe, what we did seemed like the most natural thing in the world and none of us four had any qualms about it. To me, it was like butchering a cow when I worked in the slaughterhouse. But that person was worse than an animal. No animal was capable of doing what he did. And the punishment we meted out was no crueler than the deaths he caused our people—and they had been completely innocent. I felt no emotion while we watched him die. If I thought of anything it was the gruesome killings of my father, Simcha, and Moishe the year before—also caused by an informer.

One can argue that the collaborators we executed should have been given fair trials. In an ideal world, maybe so. But we were in the forests of Volhynia, and the year was 1942. Where was the court to try them? Where was the prison to hold them? As it turned out, some of those guilty of committing genocide did not come to justice until decades after the war, and the large majority was never punished at all. Surely, while these awful crimes were being carried out against us, we had the right and the duty to take matters into our own hands.

Still, a few partisans were troubled by the moral question of whether an act of this sort had "brought us down to the level of the Nazis themselves." While I never encountered this kind of thinking in Maks' brigade, I know that at least one of Kruk's men refused, for philosophical reasons, to kill an informer in captivity. But he was hardly typical of those who fought in the forest. Almost all of us saw no ethical problem in paying back the Nazis and their accomplices in very harsh terms. Actually, it got easier each time we did it. If one hesitated in this regard I don't think he or she could have remained a fighter very long. This was neither the time nor the place for complicated debates about right and wrong. Any weakness whatsoever could prove fatal in the jungle in which we found ourselves.

No matter how we felt about the acts of reprisal we carried out, they served as a deterrent. Maks, the former editor of an underground press, made sure that word got around about why the informer we burned was executed in that manner. With printing equipment he had brought into the forest, the commander made up a dozen placards that we posted throughout the man's village the next day. They explained what had happened and threatened collective punishment should something similar occur again. Maks was not bluffing. Later in the war, responding to an act of treachery, he had some of his men burn down half a village.

His hard-line policy gradually made the countryside a safer place for Jews. The Germans often bribed the locals with food or vodka for information. We had to counter this by letting potential informers know there was a price to be paid for complicity—their lives. And an aggravated case of betrayal would be punished by an agonizing death.

By January 1943, the peasants of northern Volyhnia knew us as a force to be reckoned with. In fact, as the instances of collaboration with the Nazis declined, a number of Jews felt safe enough to come out of hiding and make their way to our civilian camp in sight of Ukrainian villagers who earlier would have turned them in for a sack of salt. There is no telling how many lives were saved in this way. It all came down to a fight against long odds, and we didn't think twice about using any means we could.

SIX

My War

WHILE WE CARRIED OUT SOME DEEDS of retaliation and revenge, our main purpose was like that of most partisans: disrupting the German war effort. For more than a year we blew up trains and railway tracks, damaged highways, bombed bridges, and cut telephone lines. We gathered intelligence on the Wehrmacht's movements and sabotaged their supply houses of food and clothing. In short, we were the biggest obstacle they faced as they tried to send men and supplies to the eastern front. Although we don't often get enough credit for it, the partisans played a critical role in the outcome of the war.

One crucial factor in our effectiveness was the arrival in late 1942 of a man who would transform us from a rag-tag band into a tough and professional fighting force. Anton Brinsky, a colonel in the Red Army, was given the daunting task of training the pro-Soviet partisan groups in north-central Volhynia, coordinating our efforts, and above all tying us to the overall war plan developed in the Kremlin. Today, a statue of him stands in Manievich.

By 1942, Stalin recognized the potential of more than a hundred thousand troops who for various reasons had remained in eastern Poland after his army's defeat there the year before. A number of them were roaming the forests in half-starved gangs bent on little more than pillage. But those who had escaped from the German POW camps or forced labor details were strongly motivated to fight the Nazis. Many others who had been in hiding the whole time, even including some deserters, were also willing to return to combat. If these men, joined by anti-fascist locals, could be properly organized, they would constitute a powerful weapon behind German lines. So when word reached Moscow that Polish and Ukrainian communists like Maks and Kruk were forming partisan bands and that left-behind Soviet soldiers in large numbers were eager to fight again, Stalin moved to take advantage of the opportunity.

Colonel Brinsky was one of several high ranking officers selected to hone the underground groups into a unified and effective military force. He had been parachuted into Belorussia, the wooded region to our northeast that was even more of a hotbed of partisan activity than Volhynia. After making contact with several camps there, he reached ours in December 1942. He brought with him a few highly trained fighters, crates of explosives and demolition equipment, and the most coveted prize of all—a powerful radio transmitter that would link us to the Soviet high command. With the radio we were able to set up airdrops that brought us medicine, guns, and ready-to-assemble bombs. Over the airwaves we could receive coded orders for our missions, as well as news of the war.

A square-jawed man with a rigid bearing, Brinsky immediately imposed strict discipline. He voiced his disapproval of the hundreds of non-combatants in our midst. In particular, the wailing children—mostly orphans as young as three—posed a major distraction since they were intermingled among the fighters. Maks pleaded with him that we had a responsibility to the civilians and that they had no other place to go. Finally, Brinsky settled the matter in the most practical way possible. We would continue to feed, clothe, and protect the civilians, but they would live separately in their own camp about two miles from the fighters. In a few cases, it meant dividing families, but at least there would still be contact between the two groups.

After helping the civilians build their own ziemlankas, we were free to focus exclusively on our military duties. Brinsky quickly laid down a series of rules and regulations. We had to rise at daybreak, strip to the waist, and wash ourselves outside even in the most frigid weather. Sometimes, when the water was poured out of the bucket it froze on my back. Although painful, it got the blood flowing in the morning. If we didn't have soap, we used sand or ashes. Brinsky forbade beards; his partisans were required to shave every day. So on our expeditions we made a point of pocketing the peasants' double-edged razor blades, which we sharpened against the inside of a drinking glass. We had to follow special procedures for the cleaning and care of our weapons; we had a tighter system of guard duty; and we were also expected to speak Russian.

These decrees were readily accepted because we knew we couldn't function as before. We needed the structure Moscow imposed on us through the colonel. In fact, we were grateful to Brinsky, affectionately calling him *Dadya Petya* (Uncle Peter). For one thing, he made it clear at the outset that he would not tolerate anti-Semitism. Except for a few jokes and stories about soft, effeminate Yeshiva boys, this had not been a problem in Maks' brigade. But another partisan commander nearby, a maniacal alcoholic named

Nasekin, actually planned to kill all the Jews in our unit as well as
Kruk's. Dadya Petya uncovered the plot, removed Nasekin, and,
we heard later, had him executed. After that, some of us wondered
if Brinsky himself might be a Jew.

It also meant a lot that this emissary from Moscow never tried
to indoctrinate us with communist ideology. Everyone understood
that we were working for Stalin, yet, unlike many other partisans,
we were not required to show any enthusiasm for him or the
Soviet motherland. There was a commissar in our camp who was
technically responsible for stating and enforcing the party line, but
his work had a low priority and most of the time he wasn't heard
from. We discussed politics, of course, but the job we had to do
was always uppermost in our minds.

Maks was given the rank of captain and remained our unques-
tioned leader because Brinsky, after several months of whipping us
into shape, was usually away overseeing Kruk's unit among half a
dozen others. But now we regarded ourselves as serving in Brinsky's *otriad*, the Russian word for partisan brigade.

Dadya Petya's chief objective was the disruption of the rail system, especially the vital line that ran from Brest-Litovsk through
the Volhynian towns of Kovel and Sarny and then all the way
to Kiev. He gave Maks a list of targets for us to hit. Maks or his
deputy and dispatcher, Dov Bronstein, known as Barku, in turn
selected teams of fighters to carry out each mission. To reach our
targets, we were sent on horseback as far as fifty miles from camp.
We rode at night to avoid detection, resting only during the day.
Barku and Maks made it clear that under no circumstances were
we to be taken alive by the enemy; we were to kill ourselves rather
than become prisoners.

Even before Brinsky's arrival we had done some damage to the
rail lines. At first, we shifted sections of track a foot or so simply

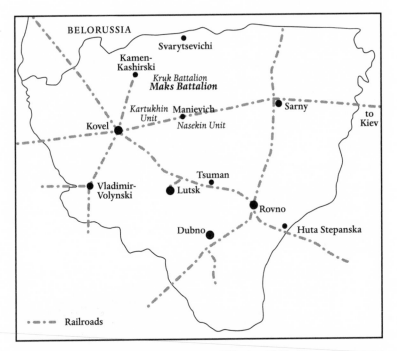

Volhynia in German-occupied Ukraine, 1942–43

by using crowbars. That would often be enough to derail the next locomotive that came along. Sometimes, with the aid of friendly peasants, we were able to remove whole sections of the track. Although we enjoyed a degree of success with these methods, the tracks and trains could be quickly repaired and unfortunately little harm came to the freight and people on board.

But some of the Russians in our camp knew how to make explosives and, with the equipment Brinsky brought, we could operate on a different level. By early 1943 we were ready to blow up the trains. Yet we faced some serious logistical difficulties. For one thing, the mines weighed over a hundred pounds and were not easy to transport long distances at night on dirt roads. A bigger problem was the primitive detonator. We would have to dig a large hole for the bomb under the tie, and string out a wire or rope hundreds of feet long. Then we'd wait for the train and at just the right moment pull the line hard to trigger the explosion. We had a pretty good idea of the schedule since friendly signalers passed along the information to Maks' agents. The railway workers knew we considered them the enemy, so quite a few hedged their bets by secretly cooperating with us. Once we learned the day and time of an oncoming train, we tried to choose a spot where the tracks came very close to the forest so we could escape easily. After making the long ride back to camp we would receive our next assignment, rest up, and a few nights later go out and cause another train wreck.

Other partisan brigades in our region were doing the same thing that winter, and the Germans quickly devised a plan of defense by stationing troops of their ally Hungary as sentries along the key rail lines between Germany and the Russian front. Every thousand yards or so there would be a Hungarian soldier, carrying a whistle or some other alarm, walking back and forth on the

A train car derailed by the partisans near Manievich

lookout for saboteurs. Our own countermeasure: We had silencers for our guns and were usually able to eliminate these watchmen before planting the mine.

We had a number of close calls. One time, on a very dark night, we had to place the bomb in a precarious spot on the rail line. It required our crossing a river by boat and climbing up a steep embankment. We dug the hole and went back to the boat to get the mine. Normally, we would have carried away the displaced dirt in a blanket or canvas sheet and filled the hollow space with gravel to make it appear as if nothing had been disturbed. But in this exposed position, with our backs to the river and lacking the protection of a nearby forest, there wasn't enough time. When we returned with the bomb and reached the top of the slope, a Hungarian guard emerged from out of the darkness walking in the direction of the hole. We knew it would be impossible for him to miss all the soil spread out alongside the tracks. He was only a few feet from us, but before we could aim our guns he walked right by the fresh mound without even changing stride. To this day I believe he saw the earth we had dug out. But at the same moment he must have realized that partisans were nearby and if he blew his whistle he'd be a dead man. As soon as he was out of sight we ran up to the track, put the bomb in the hole and covered it with gravel. And we were just in time to blow up the approaching train, before scurrying down the incline and getting back across the water in our boat.

As time went on we received better equipment. Small Soviet planes dropped boxes of explosives and detonators of a different kind, which made our job easier. We no longer needed a wire connected to the mine. The new blasting cap had a button on top that was pushed down by the depression of the rails from the weight of the oncoming train. This meant we also no longer had to remain near the target until the bomb exploded. The Germans, again, countered: At the head of each freight train the locomotive pushed a couple of open boxcars filled only with rocks. The bomb would destroy nothing of significance.

So the cat-and-mouse game continued. We reverted to the manual form of detonation, waiting for the first few cars to pass before pulling the wire or rope the instant that the locomotive—or better yet, a passenger car with German troops—passed over the mine. By then we had also received timing devices from the Red Army as well as bombs with magnetic casings. These could be attached to trains while they were still in the terminal. Although the stations were guarded, it wasn't hard for us to sneak in, crawl under a train about to depart, and slap one of those time bombs on the inside of a wheel.

By the spring of 1943, the partisan groups had crippled the entire rail network of northern Volhynia. The Germans lost a considerable number of men and a huge amount of freight and equipment. Even when we caused only minor damage to a train or the tracks, it took time for repairs and the whole system was backed up. For a while the railways became so dangerous that the military planners in Berlin shifted to roads and trucks to supply their flagging armies in Russia. So we mined the highways, too, which weren't that wide. Just one of our bombs could leave a deep crater across the whole road. It is no wonder that Hitler deployed about twenty thousand German soldiers to crush the partisan movement in Eastern Europe.

Maks and Brinsky wisely decided to avoid head-to-head combat with the Wehrmacht. Other partisan groups, driven, understandably, by feelings of revenge, directly attacked the Germans by assassinating high-ranking officers and even raiding army bases. But while they enjoyed a few spectacular successes, their own

losses were often staggering. Until the very last weeks before the liberation our policy was rather one of hit and run, enabling us to use the forest to the best advantage. This was the only prudent course given the great imbalance between them and us in numbers, equipment, and training. At the end of the day it was more important to save lives—not only our own but those in the civilian camp who were dependent on us—than to kill Germans.

This didn't mean that we would not try a well-planned ambush on occasion. One day Maks got a tip from his mole in the Manievich police station that the Germans, trying to add to their food supply, were about to go to a nearby village to seize cattle. They would be returning to town on a wagon road through thickly forested territory we knew well, and at a carefully chosen spot we waited for them. Through the trees we saw a whole procession: four peasants herding the cattle, in front of them several Ukrainian policemen and, leading the parade, three German motorcyclists, each accompanied by another soldier in a sidecar.

With grenades we blew up two of the slow-moving motorcycles along with their passengers. But the third one got away and sped into Manievich. The cattle, frightened by the explosions, turned and trotted back toward their village. Our victory was that no one came looking for us later. This incident, among others, convinced the Germans of the peril awaiting them in the woods. Early in the game they generally regarded the timberland as too dangerous and conceded it to us. This made a strong impression on many of the peasants who came to see the partisans as the ruling force. We had no government buildings and not even a flag; we printed no currency or postage stamps. But the forest north of Manievich was our country.

Morale was high among Maks' fighters. Despite the special

privileges that he and his friends received, we all felt a strong sense of camaraderie. Of course, the idea that under communism everyone was equal proved to be a myth even in the forest. The commander and his upper echelon did not live in a crowded, half-buried ziemlanka like we did but in a proper house made of thick logs and built above ground. But Maks was not one to stay inside and give orders. He mixed with his fighters at all hours of the day, and that raised our spirits. Alongside us at sunrise, he, too, would wash his upper body with ice-cold water, making jokes in the process. Often, he took his meals with us outdoors as well. Although he had first call on any vodka brought into the camp, he ate the same food as everyone else, unlike other partisan commanders. Above all, he was by our side in many of the pitched battles we fought, and on more than one occasion he was seriously wounded.

Most of my contact with him occurred in a little office in his house that he used as a war room. There he would debrief us after we returned from a mission, though it often seemed he knew what had happened even before we told him. If we accomplished our objective, he was not short on praise. When things went wrong, he could flare up in rage, but he understood the role that luck played in every operation. Seasoned partisans, who Maks knew not to be reckless or careless, were rarely bawled out.

A highly varied group, we fighters certainly had internal disagreements. But we all pulled together for the cause. As time went on, more women became combatants, ultimately constituting some fifteen percent of the fighters. There were Russians, Poles, Ukrainians, Belorussians, and Jews among us. About half of our unit consisted of former Red Army troops, but they were themselves a mixed lot. Not all of them were East Europeans; some came from the Asian part of the Soviet Union. And they had joined under

diverse circumstances, most coming voluntarily but others need-
ing some persuading. These were men who thought they could
work in peace on a secluded farm for the duration of the war.
But Maks made it clear to any of these ex-soldiers he found that
if they failed to enlist in one of the Soviet partisan brigades they
would by executed as deserters.

On the other hand, young able-bodied Jews were generally eager
to join the partisan ranks and accounted for one of every seven fighters in Volhynia, almost two thousand of the fourteen-thousand-
strong force. This was remarkably high considering that so many
Jews had been killed before the partisan phase of the war in Eastern
Europe had begun; by late 1942, Jews were only a tiny segment of
the province's population. Brinsky's otriad had the highest percentage of Jews of any partisan brigade in Volhynia. Within it, Kruk's
unit was more than a third Jewish and among Maks's roughly one
hundred fighters Jews numbered about two dozen.

There were times, especially in the beginning, when we felt that
more was expected of us than the others. Because of the deeply
ingrained stereotype of the "cowardly" Jew, or the "weak" Jew (half
a decade before the establishment of Israel began to change such
conceptions), we naturally wanted to prove to our Slavic comrades
that we were braver than they were. Most of us, therefore, were
the first to volunteer for dangerous duty. But there were other reasons, too, that Jews were generally more motivated than gentiles
were—we had more of a score to settle and, in a sense, less to lose.
Most of the non-Jews could look forward to going home after the
war. For us, it was different. We knew that our families, indeed our
entire communities, had been annihilated.

After a while, though, we were judged solely by how well we
did our jobs. Ethnic distinctions didn't count much. But something else in a person's background did mean a lot. There were

those in camp who were used to manual labor and the outdoors, and those who in their entire lives had never dirtied their hands. A man or woman who could ride a horse, shoot a rifle, and carry heavy equipment, a person who could withstand the cold and subsist on a bad diet, was a valued member of our team. Someone from the city who had been a lawyer or a scholar, say, and used to the finer things in life, was usually not suited to fighting in the forest. And of course the intellectuals were uncomfortable in an environment of heavy drinking, vulgar language, and violent behavior. Thus the partisan life reversed the status that people had in their prewar roles. There was no place for a mama's boy here. The hardened guys who set the tone were not about to indulge someone who expected the comforts of home.

Exceptions were made for several Jewish physicians, whose skills we desperately needed. One of them, Dr. Melchior from Manievich, had been reluctant to join us early on. Maks tried personally to lure him out of the ghetto before the liquidation, and he refused. Later, however, he escaped and served as our doctor until the liberation, saving countless lives of both fighters and civilians. But he put on airs as a member of the intelligentsia, thinking he deserved better because he was a professional person. He wouldn't even go outside at night to urinate like the rest of us. He thought it was more refined to pee in a bottle that he kept close by. We all made fun of him behind his back.

Although in temperament I was mild and quiet compared with most of the fighters, I quickly adapted to the culture of the partisans and fit right in. My boyhood in Biala Podlaska provided me with the best preparation I could have had for the woods. I was especially close to two men who were also no strangers to rural life. Isaac Guz and Moniek Berensztejn had both grown up in villages in north-central Volhynia. Trading with the peasants, they got to know not only many of the inhabitants in the countryside, but also the tricky terrain of swamps and bogs. Even in a thick fog, yet another perennial problem in the region, they could safely find their way back to camp on unmarked forest trails.

Guz, around forty, was in our unit before I arrived and took a fatherly interest in me. Like Tateh, he had worked as a butcher. Tall and well-built, Guz was a calm man who performed his duties with precision. No matter how dangerous the situation, he never lost his composure. Berensztejn and his sister Museya, who was also a fighter, came to us from another brigade. Moniek was just a few years older than I and more excitable than Guz, but like him highly capable and reliable.

Not yet twenty years old, I was considered too young to head a mission. But beginning in 1943, Guz and Berensztejn served as leaders and almost always I was with one or both of them. Our team of four (only one of the many groups simultaneously sent out by Maks) was generally rounded out by one or two Russians. Everyone understood that the various elements of partisan tactics were best served by the units being as small as possible.

There were other brave Jews in the forest—Berek, who for some unknown reason we called "the Colonel," Brat, Kramer, and Krawiec. The Russian Varsniak, who had studied for the priesthood, and the tough Ukrainian girl Froska were no less dependable. The teamwork that we had was extraordinary; on missions we worked together as one. I trusted them with my life, and they trusted me with theirs. They became my new family, and there was no better feeling in the world than to return from a successful mission with everyone safe.

As 1943 dawned, things began to jell. With the newly built ziemlankas protecting us from the cold, the peasants providing us with food, and the civilians seeing to our daily needs, we could survive in the forest. And with the military aid brought by Brinsky and the airdrops of explosives, we had the ability to hurt the Germans badly by derailing their trains.

But in mid-January we received a threat to our very existence. Maks learned from his well-placed intelligence sources that the Germans were about to raid the camp. They amassed more than three thousand soldiers joined by numerous Ukrainian nationalist gangs, in all a force ten times the number of fighters in the entire Brinsky brigade.

There was no choice but to move deeper into the forest. And, once again, Maks was forced by other partisan commanders, such as the anti-Semitic Kartukhin, to defend the wisdom of maintaining such a large civilian camp. How could the fighters retreat, Kartukhin reproached him, with the burden of so many non-combatants in tow? But it was obvious to Maks and everyone else that to abandon the civilians now was to issue them death sentences. Fortunately, Brinsky sided with Maks and his allies, who now included Kruk, and the decision was made to evacuate everyone.

Maks had been warned more than a week in advance, and we used the time to gather horses and sleds, as well as boots and heavy clothing from the nearby villages and estates. But the weather turned bitterly cold, and we were faced with a trek, in temperatures as low as fifteen below zero Fahrenheit, some thirty miles to a spot just short of the Belorussian border.

Before we left camp we made snowmen, dressed them in old clothes and put sticks that looked like rifles in their hands. I can't recall if they were intended to be decoys, or if to relieve the tension we were simply amusing ourselves. We found out later that the Germans shot at them.

At midnight we left our forest home, an exodus of five hundred people, some of whom had to travel the ice-covered paths on foot. Our destination was the village of Svarytsevichi, due north, where the civilians could be housed in an abandoned school and where other partisan groups would join us. Although it wasn't snowing, it was the coldest weather I've ever endured. For an extra bit of warmth, many tied rags around the outside of their boots.

An element of Brinsky's plan was to deploy a hundred partisans near our vacated camp to harry the invaders. I set out on the journey north, among the guards escorting the civilians, but twenty-four hours later Maks ordered a group of us to head back to reinforce the fighters that had been left behind.

In the bone-chilling woods we had skirmishes with the Germans and fought full-scale battles against Ukrainian partisans. These were the Banderovtsky, bloodthirsty bands who took the name of their fanatic young leader, Stepan Bandera, the son of a priest. In their blind hatred of the Soviet Union and the Jews, their philosophy was similar to that of National Socialism and initially they thought of Hitler as a savior. But as time went on, and the Germans treated the Ukrainian population with increasing brutality and refused to award them statehood, the Banderovtsky had some armed clashes with the Wehrmacht. Still, their main enemy by far was the Soviet partisan movement and they tried to ambush us whenever they could, even as we went out on missions of sabotage against the Nazis. They also hunted down Jewish refugees and attacked ethnic Poles who had their own nationalist ambitions.

Now, under the cover of the German assault, the Banderovtsky came after us in force. They recruited hundreds of well-armed policemen and were actually more formidable than the Wehrmacht because they knew the forest well. We prevailed against them in that battle, but we would have to fight them again and again until our liberation more than a year later.

The Germans withdrew from the woods with little success. Their army, dependent on tanks and trucks to cover ground quickly, was not geared for a campaign against guerrilla warfare, particularly on the forbidding terrain of northern Volhynia. They would be wary of entering the forest again.

We fighters came back to our camp within a few days. Luckily, the intense cold eased and the return trip for the civilians, more than a week after they had left, was less arduous. We were amazed to find that although the Germans had overrun our base, they had not demolished it. It gave us a new feeling of confidence to know that while we had had to retreat, we could retake possession of our forest sanctuary.

The news coming over the radio lifted our hopes even higher. The German Sixth Army, encircled at Stalingrad, had surrendered and a quarter of a million Nazi soldiers were killed, wounded, or taken prisoner. The image we had of the Red Army, and even Stalin as a military leader, improved dramatically. As the first signs

Some of Maks' fighters in mid-1943. Isaac Guz is toward the right, facing the camera, with belts across his chest

of spring arrived in the forest, our feeling was that the tide had turned in the east. We were still frustrated that America and Britain had not yet invaded the continent and established a "second front," but now we felt that Hitler was going to lose the war. It was just a matter of time.

Increasing amounts of air-dropped equipment came our way. A field would be selected that we would illuminate with a fire in each corner so the pilot, in radio contact with us, could see the location for the drop. Later, we were bold enough to build a small runway. The pilot would not only land, but also climb out and talk to us. In exchange for a wristwatch, say, he might trade one of us something special, like a sleek, new revolver that was not part of the official shipment. On occasion he would return to his base with a sick or wounded partisan in need of more medical help than we could provide.

After the spring thaw in 1943, Maks' attention shifted to the plight of his own countrymen. The Banderovtsky had sharply escalated their war against the Polish minority and put the torch to entire villages. Realizing that their former German allies would likely be defeated, the Ukrainians feared that following the war the USSR would return Volhynia to Poland, an intolerable solution in their eyes. By committing atrocities against the Poles throughout the province, the Banderovtsky hoped to provoke a mass flight of refugees westward across the Bug River and thus tilt the demographic balance further in their favor: "ethnic cleansing," as we'd call it today. The Ukrainians especially resented the Poles whom the government in Warsaw had settled in Volhynia in the 1920s and 1930s, and this group was singled out for wholesale slaughter.

It was no surprise that in the face of such carnage Maks refused to remain a bystander. His policy of saving Jewish civilians was now regarded a success by the other unit leaders and by brigade commander Brinsky. With little debate this time they all agreed to come to the aid of the Poles. Although I was not part of the detachment that was sent, a partisan force under the command of Maks' trusted deputy, Dov Bronstein, went about eighty miles southeast of our camp to defend against a Banderovtsky attack on a village, Huta Stepanska, where many Polish refugees had fled. Our men fought side by side with the *Armia Krajowa,* the Polish underground that constituted yet another partisan movement in a forest that by this time was almost crowded. Known as the Home Army, the Polish fighters had nationalist aims exactly opposite the Ukrainians: they were desperately trying to save Volhynia for Poland. (As it turned out, of course, both they and the Banderovtsky would be bitterly disappointed: Volhynia *was* made a part of the Ukraine after the war, but the entire "republic" would be firmly in the iron cage of the Soviet Union for nearly the next half century. Only in 1991 did it become an independent state.) The Home Army had been fairly dormant in our region until mid-1943, but the killing raids of the Banderovtsky led them to take up arms.

I don't believe anyone in our unit was enthusiastic about Polish nationalism. Even Maks himself, a Pole but a dedicated communist, probably put the political interests of the Soviet Union ahead of those of the land of his birth. We Jews had mixed feelings about this mission because the Home Army was anti-Semitic. It had rejected many Jewish men and women who were qualified to enter its ranks. But in this time of shifting alliances, we joined them to fight a common enemy that was bent on mass murder. Our men and the Armia Krajowa sustained heavy losses but in the end drove the Banderovtsky away. Then Maks was able to perform his second great humanitarian act of the war. He arranged an armed escort for several hundred Poles to be brought out of Huta Ste-panska and he sheltered them in a civilian camp not far from our own. Here, they lived under our protection until the liberation.

Our military goal also changed in the latter part of 1943 as the Red Army scored more and more victories and drove the Nazi invaders out of the USSR and back toward Germany. Earlier, our job had been to slow the German juggernaut by cutting their long supply lines to the eastern front. Now that the Soviets were suc-ceeding with their massive counteroffensive, our task was to block, or at least harass, the Wehrmacht as it retreated homeward. The Germans would then be cut to ribbons by the relentless Red Army assault. Along the huge front that stretched from the Baltic Sea in the north to the Black Sea in the south the Soviets penetrated most deeply in the center, not far from where we were operat-ing. They established a bulge—military historians refer to it as a "salient"—that by autumn of 1943 was only a couple of hundred miles away. With the liberation of Kiev in early November, it was clear that the front was rapidly moving back towards us. As we prepared for the winter, my second in the forest, everyone spoke of a huge battle looming in which we would have a hand.

But a careless act on my part almost caused me to miss the action. On our way back from a routine mission, five of us settled in for the night at a friendly farmhouse. As usual, one of our team stood guard. He was to be relieved after a two-hour shift, during which Guz and I and two others slept. For some reason I broke one of the cardinal rules of the partisans and removed my boots. Nor was I even wearing socks. The custom in Volhynia was simply to wrap a square cloth around each of your feet before putting on your footwear.

Sure enough, we were attacked by a German patrol, which was rare in those remote parts. Hearing gunshots, we woke up and looked out the window. Our comrade was desperately trying to hold them off, thereby buying us a little time.

But they shot him dead and were now charging the house. Our only hope was to run—barefoot in my case—out the back door. Putting on those tight-fitting boots would have cost precious minutes I couldn't afford. The snow wasn't deep enough to hinder us, and the woods began less than fifty yards from the house, so we could get away. Some volleys were fired in our direction, but the Germans didn't pursue us.

Naturally, by the time we got to the next village most of my toes were frostbitten. I could neither walk nor put on shoes because of the swelling. We were also deeply concerned about what the Nazis would do to the sympathetic farmer who had sheltered us. We found out later they believed his story that we'd taken over his house at gunpoint.

There was no choice but for me to remain a while with one of the locals. Like so many in that region, the peasant baked his own bread and behind his big oven was a warm space that felt like paradise. This is where I hid and convalesced and thought a lot about the home I once had in Biala Podlaska. To reduce the swelling, the old man used an ancient remedy: He applied goose fat and swaddled my feet in rags. In about a week I was healed and could return to camp. This Ukrainian took good care of me, and in doing so risked his life. But we were not about to rely on his decency alone. Guz and the others made sure he understood that if I were harmed he would pay the highest price.

In the first days of 1944, the Red Army entered the northeastern corner of Volhynia. Their infantry came in behind large T-34 tanks with wide treads that had good traction. They also had American trucks and seemingly no shortage of gasoline. When the terrain required it, they would press into service the peasants' high-wheeled horse-drawn carts. It was hard to believe this was the same army that two and a half years earlier had collapsed overnight.

In a few weeks they turned south and moved toward the main city of the province, Rovno. Almost every Soviet partisan brigade in northern and central Volhynia headed toward Rovno, too, more than ten thousand fighters in all. Our mission turned out to be even more difficult and dangerous than we had thought. We were ordered not only to hinder the probable Wehrmacht retreat, but also to attack fortified German positions from the west while Soviet troops and tanks came at them from the east. This showdown would decide the fate of our region.

The target assigned to Brinsky's brigade was the key village of Tsuman, which commanded the main road to Rovno, less than thirty miles away. In Tsuman the Germans had brick fortifications, high-caliber machine guns, and two thousand soldiers. Sobering as this was, we felt pride in having "graduated." Many of us now had automatic weapons. I had recently gotten the same kind of sixty-round submachine gun Maks carried. New disks of ammunition could quickly and easily be inserted, so I was capable of generating a great deal of firepower. We had fixed machine guns as well, and an array of cannons and grenade launchers. After almost a year and a half of hit-and-run actions, we were finally considered ready to face the Germans head on as if we were regulars in the Red Army.

But the battle turned out to be a horror. Communication broke down between the Red Army and us, as well as among the various partisan groups. The Soviet troops unexpectedly delayed their march on Rovno, allowing the Germans to bring more men, artillery, and planes toward Tsuman than we anticipated. Even the weather turned against us. It was unseasonably warm at the end of January and the bogs and swamps were not frozen solid but rather mud and mush. This did not impede the Wehrmacht, which moved on the main roads. But it slowed us down terribly as we tried to get our wounded out of the line of fire and back into the safety of the forest. We lost many good people.

The ensuing chaos remains in my mind as much as the terror. It began with my unit just outside the gateway to Tsuman, guarding the highway to the east. This was the route, it was feared, through which the Germans would bring in more troops. Meanwhile, two other units under Brinsky's command broke into the heavily fortified village and heroically captured almost a dozen German bunkers. But heading into the center of Tsuman, the partisans suddenly found themselves encircled. Most of our unit was ordered to come to their aid.

I was one of only twenty fighters left guarding the road. Our objective was to hold off the German battalion already on its way from Rovno. Our leader was my buddy Moniek Berensztejn, who directed us first to mine the highway and then set up big machine guns on both sides of it. As we worked furiously, we spotted in the distance the German column coming toward us. We had just enough time to hide behind the trees. Our mines destroyed the two trucks in the lead but there were many other vehicles behind them. Over a hundred German soldiers jumped out and charged us—directly into our heavy machine gun fire. We ran into the forest and, uncharacteristically, they gave chase. Although they surrounded us in an open field, we held out until, miraculously, our comrades returned from Tsuman in time to surprise the enemy from behind. Our men broke the German grip on us, forcing them back into their trucks.

By dusk, the fighting died down and we rested during the

night in ditches atop a nearby ridge. Just as the sun was coming up the next morning we suddenly realized that not all the Germans had left the woods. Seven had lost their way and by mistake stumbled right into our temporary encampment. Completely unaware, they walked uphill towards us. Our guards easily got the jump on them and a few of us Jews joined the small force that held them at gunpoint. We ordered them to drop their weapons and raise their hands over their heads, and they quickly complied. I think they figured, with some relief actually, that they would spend the rest of the war as POWs. Maks, who was hurrying somewhere else, immediately grasped what had happened and the opportunity it presented. On the run, he yelled to us, "We need their uniforms!"

We understood that he meant much more. About ten of us forced them, two or three at a time, into a ravine not far from where we had made camp. We brought along guns with silencers. When they were told that some of us were Jewish, I saw their faces drop. Then we ordered them to undress. If our German sounded a bit like Yiddish, it was all the better. They took off their uniforms and remained standing in their underwear, shaking with fear. We said, "*Alles*." And there they were, "Aryan Supermen," their naked flesh trembling exactly the same way millions of Jews did before they were killed. We felt almost euphoric to have the chance to avenge the deaths of our loved ones. It was like a gift. I heard Simcha's voice say, "Good for you, Yosel." Although we had already killed scores of German troops by then, these were the first we put to death looking directly into their eyes. Even if I had any doubt about executing those soldiers, I don't know what the alternative would have been. There was absolutely no way to take prisoners in the midst of that week-long battle.

Soon, some of our men and women dressed up in the German uniforms we'd gotten and calmly walked close enough to their camp to throw in a few grenades and take out a machine gun or two. One time a German field-kitchen was blown up, and all they lost was a vat of soup. But there was always a danger in using such a disguise since you could easily be shot by another partisan or a Soviet soldier.

Postponing for a few days our plans to capture Tsuman, and for that matter Rovno, we headed back through the wet woods hoping to meet the Red Army further north. It had also failed to attain its goal. Although the Wehrmacht was everywhere, we continued our tactics of blowing up their vehicles and using our machine guns to cut down any survivors. If it was a long column, though, we made a point of not sticking around too long. We had the upper hand in battle with small pockets of Germans that had been forced off the main roads and were wandering in the woods.

Yet for all of the experience we had gained by this point, we suffered heavy losses as we withdrew from the Tsuman-Rovno area. About a tenth of our fighters had been seriously wounded, and it was nearly impossible to carry them over ground that now resembled quicksand. Many of our horses, exhausted, hungry, and unable to find footing, proved useless. Some of our men had to harness themselves to the carts bearing the wounded. A number of partisans actually drowned in the swamps. I was in a forward position and didn't witness it, but Maks, bringing up the rear, had to beat a Jewish partisan with a stick to get the tired man to cross one of the bogs. This ragged retreat was the darkest moment in the history of the Brinsky brigade.

Finally, after days of inaction, the Soviets resumed their offensive and launched a powerful drive on Rovno. It completely altered the balance of power in the area because the Germans, forced to divert their forces eastward to meet the mighty attack, were more dispersed. We could turn around and try again to take the city. In the ensuing confusion of battle, some in our unit were actually shot, though fortunately not killed, by Red Army men mistaking them for Banderovtsky. At this stage, it was hard just knowing who was who.

But this time we made it. We entered Rovno alongside regular Soviet troops on February 5, 1944, and liberated the largest city in the province. Although we fought on the outskirts of town, we found no resistance in the center since the Germans had evacuated downtown Rovno before we arrived. For the first time in more than two and a half years I was neither under Nazi rule nor behind German lines. I had come out of the fire alive. I had fought, and I had survived.

The Brinsky otriad, along with most of the other partisan groups of Volhynia, was disbanded in Rovno. Maks, however, continued the fight. With a few trusted aides he would be parachuted west, beyond the Bug River, to form a new unit in central Poland. He would recruit most of his fighters there, largely ethnic Poles, and organize them into a group named Grunwald for the great victory his country had won over German invaders in the Middle Ages. Maks was also successful in his second campaign, and after the war was hailed as a hero. Reverting to his real name, Jozef Sobiesiak, he rose in the ranks of the Polish armed services and ultimately became a rear admiral in the navy.

Our unit, composed mostly of Russians and Jews, ceased to exist. Somewhat reluctantly we turned our weapons over to the Red Army. Our camps in the forest had also been liberated by this time and, with the Soviets in control of eastern Volhynia, it was safe for the civilians to journey to Rovno. There, they reunited with the fighters for the last time, sought information from the authorities about their families, and learned the status of their

Maks in command of the Grunwald Brigade in Poland in 1944

hometowns. From Rovno the civilians went their separate ways and before long were dispersed throughout Europe.

We fighters were all called together for a farewell meeting in the Rovno military barracks, at which time Soviet military officials thanked us for our service to the motherland. They noted our courage and skill under the most difficult conditions. But instead of receiving some sort of an "honorable discharge," I was distressed to learn that we were now all required to enlist in the regular army. "The war is not over," they solemnly declared. "Fascism in not yet dead. And all of you still have a big job ahead."

I wasn't expecting a medal or a vacation by the sea, but this news was hard to bear. It seemed that no matter what you did, it wasn't enough. I certainly had the physical strength to go on, but given that our brigade had made such a large contribution to the war effort, I honestly believed they would figure we had already done our part. Weighing on me even more was that I was the sole survivor of a large family. At the time I didn't know that in other countries, like the United States, losing your closest relatives in the war entitled you to a draft deferment or a discharge. I simply thought that since I was the only Epelbaum left, the fair thing would be to let me out of the service.

Isaac Guz and Moniek Berensztejn, who had also suffered enormous personal losses, felt the same way. For the time being, the three of us decided to move into a house in Rovno to think things over. Because the Jewish community had been destroyed, there were many vacancies despite the fact that an influx of refugees had already begun. Except for the week I spent recovering from frostbite, this was the first time any of us had lived in a proper dwelling in years. We had plenty to eat since the Soviet forces had a surplus of rations they distributed to the local population. It was American food, cans of pork and beans.

Meanwhile, the Germans regrouped further west. The front, which ran through the city of Kovel, was about sixty miles from us. There, the Wehrmacht made a determined stand and, astonishingly, it would take almost six more months before the rest of Volhynia would be liberated. The fighting in mid-1944 between the two titanic armies was even bloodier than the battle around Rovno. Guz, Berensztejn, and I witnessed a steady stream of crowded Soviet troop trains heading toward Kovel and returning to Rovno full of dead and wounded infantrymen.

Of course we wanted the Nazi regime to be demolished. But now we were beginning to have some doubts about Moscow's war aims and strategy, too. Were they just trying to defeat Hitler, or carve out an empire for themselves? The Soviets seemed to exercise no caution when it came to throwing their soldiers into battle, something that became even clearer to us by summer when they sacrificed everything in a mad race to get to Berlin before the Allies. Maybe they wouldn't rest until communism triumphed everywhere in Europe.

None of us had enjoyed living under Stalin's rigid regime between the fall of 1939 and the summer of 1941. Now we felt that we didn't deserve to be used as cannon fodder. And even if we joined the Red Army, and were lucky enough to survive, there was no guarantee we would ever be allowed to leave the "workers' paradise."

Having just emerged from a long period during which our lives had been on the line every day, there was no "great cause" that would make us give up the precious fruits of peace we were beginning to taste. Surely it was not Soviet patriotism. We three decided to remain in Rovno and avoid the recruiting officer. The majority of former partisans, including most of our unit, did join the Red Army. But our war was over.

I turned twenty that spring. In liberated Rovno, beginning to stir with new life, the world looked full of promise to me, a young man lucky to be alive. But I wasn't ready to make any real plans for the future. I still lived from one day to the next, and I was about to put myself in danger again, this time unnecessarily. I was out of the partisans, but it would not be so simple to shed the partisan way of life.

SEVEN

A Strange Freedom

OVER THE NEXT THREE AND A HALF YEARS my life lacked any real structure or direction. I wasn't a fighter in the forest anymore, but neither was I a productive member of society. It was a wild existence that I lived, operating on the edge of the law—frequently outside the law—running back and forth across a continent that, like me, was badly scarred and unsure about its prospects. It felt like I had only one foot on the ground and the other always up in the air.

I don't know if this was a dangerous form of escape, a way to avoid thinking about my past and my future, or if it was just the recklessness of a kid in his early twenties who wanted to make up for lost time. More than anything, that chaotic period was an extension of what I had experienced in Maks' brigade: constantly being on the run, doing whatever was needed for survival, and even continuing to take revenge. One or more of my former comrades were always close by during these postpartisan years, and I even wore the same Soviet officer's coat I had gotten in the fall of 1942.

The rules and regulations that had anchored my life as a partisan—the strong authority wielded by Maks and his deputies—were gone. So was the deadly enemy that you always had to worry about, lurking beyond the trees. While my mind was still in turmoil from everything that had happened, and my body craved the physical pleasures I'd been denied, nothing remained anymore to curb my behavior.

The craziness began in Rovno as we literally "dodged" the draft in February 1944. With every able-bodied young man subjected to conscription, Guz, Berensztejn, and I stayed in our apartment as much as we could. When we had to go out for food or medicine, we scanned the street for police or soldiers, and if we saw a man in uniform we'd head in the opposite direction. One time, as I was turning a corner, I came face to face with a military policeman. Fortunately I had the presence of mind to blurt out, "Which way to the recruiting center?" He pointed out the direction, but of course I ran elsewhere as soon as I was out of his sight.

We were lucky that one of our best friends in Maks' unit, Varsniak, was soon appointed by the Soviet occupying forces as the chief official for the whole city. He provided us with the papers we needed not only to move freely around Rovno but also to travel out of town. They were documents that identified us as members of Maks' new group—an elite force of commandos that was about to be parachuted behind the German lines. In reality, Maks had not selected us for this top-secret mission and he and his men had already left Rovno. But we inherited the papers of that unit and with it high status.

Now we began to enjoy life in Rovno. We had a good number of friends around because many former inhabitants of the civilian camp stopped for a while in the newly liberated city before moving on. Other Jews and non-Jews, many of whom had been in hiding during the occupation, also converged on Rovno. There was no shortage of food, drink, or entertainment in the evening and often the partying got out of hand. Rowdy drunks could be seen everywhere. As a partisan, I dared not swallow more than an ounce of vodka because I saw how dangerous it could be if you lost your vigilance. Now I could drink as much as I wanted. For the first time I really let loose.

The three of us spent a lot of time with several of the young women who had been partisan fighters and who remained in town when our unit disbanded. I became intimate with a girl named Malka, and it wasn't long before Guz, Berensztejn, and other friends started pressuring me to marry her. But all that did was make me run the other way and seek out others. At that point I was at such loose ends, not having a clue where I would end up, that I couldn't imagine myself with the responsibility of a wife and children. Finally relieved of the daily stress I felt in the partisans, I wanted nothing more than to live for the moment.

In June, still hanging out in Rovno, we learned of the Allied invasion at Normandy. If we had any doubts about a swift end to the war, they were now erased. But there was no joyous moment at that time that wasn't mixed with deep sorrow. And in trying to come to terms with what had happened, I felt the need to return to Biala Podlaska. In late summer, after the Red Army finally liberated the western bank of the Bug River, it was possible to do so.

Guz and Berensztejn traveled with me. At my urging we made one stop along the way—Manievich, the town that Maks had barred us from entering for security reasons. Although we only remained a few days in that place of hellish memories, I didn't need much time to do something I had promised myself for two years. First, I discreetly asked around if that snake who had betrayed my family was still living in the same house. Then, shortly before our train was scheduled to depart at midnight on the third day, I told my two friends that I would meet them at the railway station. I needed to take care of this on my own. In the darkness, with a can of gasoline, and a hand grenade I'd kept from my partisan days, I walked to his house. I poured the gas around the perimeter, put a match to it, and tossed the grenade through a window. It didn't feel that different from attacking a Ukrainian police headquarters when I was with Maks.

After the explosion went off, and the flames rose, I walked casually to the station. I never found out the extent of the damage, but I figure it was severe. I arrived as the train was about to leave, and the suspicious Guz, who had heard the blast, naturally wanted to know where I'd been. But it would be some time before I would tell even him.

Survivors of the concentration camps rarely took revenge in this manner. They usually did not have the opportunity or the weapons after they were liberated, and they were often too weak or sick to carry out such a deed. And having been penned in like animals, beaten, and humiliated in every way, they frequently lost the will to fight back. For us partisans it was just the opposite. Armed retaliation was second nature. My brigade had disbanded, and I was no longer behind enemy lines, but to me that counted for nothing.

We hurried aboard a westbound troop-train. I was now wearing something even better than the naval officer's dress coat: a full Red Army uniform, complete with hat, that had been mine for the taking in Rovno. My two buddies were similarly attired. But as soon as the train began to move, we noticed that we were attracting a lot of attention, the last thing I needed in light of what I had done less than a half-hour earlier. This was a Soviet military transport, all right, but carrying a battalion made up almost entirely of Asians.

The infantrymen in our car—they might have been Mongolians—eyed us with suspicion. And no matter how harmless and inoffensive we tried to appear, they became increasingly agitated. Clearly there was no use trying to banter with them in Yiddish. But neither was it easy to communicate with them in any of the other languages we knew. Yet we comprehended the basic question they were asking: "Who the hell are you?" We tried to convey the story about parachuting behind enemy lines but got nowhere. Either they didn't believe it or didn't understand it. After pointing at us and speaking loudly among themselves, one of them went to get their commanding officer.

He was a Russian and before we could utter a word he said that we would be turned over to the Soviet authorities at the last stop before the Bug, Brest-Litovsk. That city was now an important line of demarcation since Stalin was in the process of annexing Volhynia, and indeed all the territory in eastern Poland and the Baltic States the Red Army had seized in 1939 and 1940. The rest of Poland, though largely occupied by Soviet troops, figured to be an independent country. But for me to see it again, I would have to survive an interrogation.

After the train pulled into the town where my family had fled almost five years earlier, several Asian soldiers escorted us to the office of the chief of the border patrol. In the early morning light, we took out the documents we had been given six months before in Rovno. Would they carry any weight with this Soviet officer? I was not too worried he would connect me to what had just happened back in Manievich, but the three of us could be in deep trouble anyway. Everyone knew that people were sent to Siberia for a lot less than evading the draft, traveling with invalid papers, and impersonating Red Army men. We tried not to show our fear as he sat at his desk and carefully read the text.

Suddenly he stood up and saluted us! He called in several of his men, uncorked a bottle of vodka, and proceeded to toast us as heroes of the Soviet Union. We looked at each other, smiled, and joined in the celebration with gusto. We were happier than they could ever know. The officer, still singing our praises, arranged for an army truck to take us over the Bug and the twenty-five miles to Biala Podlaska.

As I looked out the window at the familiar landscape it all came back to me, the feelings of both sadness and relief when the Soviets evacuated my family in late October 1939. The seven of us had ridden east in a military vehicle on this very road. I was fifteen years old then. Now, at twenty, I was the only one to return.

Almost every other Jew was gone as well. We had been a vibrant community of around seventy-five hundred before the war, and I was soon to learn that there were perhaps two dozen Jews left. It wasn't hard to find the survivors. Mostly single people in their twenties or thirties, they all lived together in a rooming house on one large floor above a drugstore in the center of town. We three moved in there, too, and I am certain that if there had been any other Jews in Biala Podlaska we would have known about them. In the main square we'd approach anyone who we thought might be Jewish and whisper *"amcha,"* a well-known Hebrew word meaning "common people" or "folk." Yet we rarely received an affirmative answer. When we did, that person would be invited over to our little compound.

More Jews would straggle in during the next year and a half, a few of them death camp survivors. Most of the returnees, however, were those who had fled to the Soviet zone in 1939, but, unlike my family, had the good fortune to work in the mines and factories of central Asia. Yet even by the middle of 1946, when the Jewish population of Biala Podlaska hit its postwar "peak," it barely reached two hundred.

The small group we found when we arrived in August 1944 contained several former partisans like ourselves, but it consisted mainly of Jews who had been in hiding, in the countryside or in town, or who had passed as Polish Catholics. One of the latter was Helenka Rosenzweig, a pretty blond whose family had been well-off before the war. After the German invasion the Nazis killed her father. But she, her mother, and two sisters fled to Warsaw, where they lived outside the ghetto as Aryans. Helenka, knowing that almost all of her family members with the exception of her father had survived, was confident and upbeat.

This was not the case for many of the others who were physically ill and deeply depressed. Noah Rodzinek, a thirty-year-old who had been a friend of Simcha's, lost his parents, sister, and all but one of his nine brothers. Noah was hidden by a peasant late in the occupation after working for almost a year in a prison camp run by the Gestapo in Biala Podlaska. There, he was forced to bury the bodies of executed men and women in mass graves.

Another who lived with us, Leibl Hofman, had been taken from the ghetto in nearby Mezritch and put in a boxcar to Treblinka. En route, he and several others jumped off the speeding death train, only to be beaten, robbed, and stripped by Polish thugs who turned most of the escapees over to the Nazis. Hofman somehow broke away and hid in the woods. Of a family of eight children he was the only survivor.

As we reflected on our suffering and realized the extent of our losses, some went to pieces. It was not unusual to see people talking to themselves or just staring into space for hours at a time. Several developed nervous tics and twitches. Everyone bled from the heart.

Although I, too, was the sole survivor of a large family, I was not mired in gloom like most of the others. My service in the partisans had afforded me an outlet for my anger. So, along with

Guz and Berensztejn, I tried as best I could to bring a bit of hope and cheer into the place. Every evening our group sat around a big table together for dinner. Although the war still raged less than a hundred miles from us, it was not difficult to find good food. We ate roast chicken or geese, consumed a lot of vodka, and talked late into the night. We were like a large Jewish family—the only one left in Biala Podlaska.

Naturally we struggled to understand what had occurred. Because many of the people there had grown up in pious families, the discussion often turned to God. But few still clung to their former beliefs, and there was scant observance among us of the Sabbath or kosher laws. A few survivors, their lives having been spared at the last possible moment, were convinced that divine intervention was the only reason they were still alive. I drew just the opposite conclusion. Where they saw the mighty hand of the Lord, I saw simply the luck of the draw. It was circumstance that

Almost all of the surviving Jews of Biala Podlaska in the fall of 1944, bravely smiling for the camera. Helenka and I are seated on the right, leaning in.

saved me. I could have been killed as easily as a fly being swatted. I had rebelled against Orthodoxy as a child and now, given the enormity of the catastrophe, what little faith I had was extinguished. Most of the others felt the same way. Even those who continued to believe in Him voiced their anger, their bitterness that He had let this happen.

And our punishment still wasn't over. We huddled together not only for emotional support but also for safety, fearful of our Polish neighbors. They had brutally attacked a number of returning Jews, and each of us felt that he or she could be next. Toward the end of 1944 Poles pulled a pregnant Jewish woman out of a railway car and beat her to death; she had survived a concentration camp. Then five Jews from nearby Yanova, my mother's hometown, were murdered by a mob. All of this was merely the beginning of a wave of violence that took the lives of more than fifteen hundred Jews across the country by the summer of 1947, triggering an exodus to Palestine and the United States. The Germans killed ninety percent of Polish Jewry; the anti-Semitic outrages that followed resulted in the migration of two thirds of the remnant that had survived.

Even the dead were not immune to Polish hatred. In mid-1946, long after I had left Biala Podlaska, Rodzinek, Hofman, and other survivors erected a monument to the Jewish victims of the town. The memorial, near a common grave, was vandalized and later destroyed by hooligans. Around that time, after two Jewish youths were killed by Poles, virtually all the remaining Jews pulled out of town, most of them migrating to Germany, which they considered safer than their native land.

Early on, of course, we had no way of knowing how bad this postliberation period was going to be. In the fall of 1944, even before Warsaw was liberated, the committee that would soon declare itself the provisional Polish government denounced anti-

Semitism and even placed a number of Jews in top posts. Most of us were pleased to see this communist group, organized by Moscow, gain the upper hand. It seemed much better than the alternative, the right-wing London-based Polish Government-in-Exile and its Home Army, both of which were filled with Jew-haters.

So there were some idealists in the Jewish community, shattered though it was, who saw a bright future for a Poland that would be both socialist and democratic. This was the thinking of my older cousins, Sarah and Gittel, both communists, who had fled to the Soviet Union in 1939, received further indoctrination there, and now returned to Poland as mid-level functionaries in the provisional administration. They worked in another town but came back to visit Biala Podlaska for a tearful reunion when we hugged tightly—my only surviving relatives in the country. Even in the face of all the destruction around them, they were optimistic. The goal they had been working toward their entire lives was now in reach, they told me—a People's Republic of Poland that would ensure the equality and the acceptance of the Jews.

I was not impressed. What really counted for me was the look in the eyes of the man on the street. The deep-seated anti-Jewish attitudes that had been so prevalent in the late 1930s had only been inflamed by five years of Nazi propaganda. And the installation of Jews in high places by the Soviet-backed government actually hurt us on the local level because the Poles bitterly resented the influence of "Stalin's Jewish puppets." As in 1939, when, faced with the Nazi invasion, we openly welcomed the arrival of the Red Army, we were once again accused of helping the enemy and of being disloyal to Poland.

I felt uneasy on the streets of the town where I had grown up. Everywhere, I wore my Red Army uniform to give people the impression that I was a Soviet soldier. It was much safer than

In Biala Podlaska, late 1944

being a returning Jewish survivor. I recognized a few of the non-Jews in town, people with whom my family had done business when I was a boy. But the last thing I was going to do was run up and say, "Remember me? I'm Yosel Epelbaum, the son of Hershko the butcher." All my instincts told me to keep a low profile.

It took a long while before I had the emotional strength to return to our old apartment house. It was devastating enough to see what had become of the town square that had been so full of life before the war. Nearly all the shops had been Jewish-owned, and now they were vacant. Commercial life was dead.

When I finally made my way to Ulica Yatkova 14 I saw several Polish families—complete strangers—in my family's building. It looked to me as if they felt perfectly at home. All I did was stare at them in silence. Now, as I thought of Tateh and Mameh, Simcha, Sima, Sol, and Moishe, of the life we led and the business we had, I was overwhelmed by a loneliness that penetrated my bones. I stood on the street where I had walked every day of my childhood and wept. Despite everything I had been through, it was only now that I fully grasped the magnitude of the disaster.

EIGHT

Flimflam Man

I REMAINED IN BIALA PODLASKA for nearly half a year, until early 1945 when the Germans were driven almost completely out of Poland and I could move further west. It was a time of mourning and also a period when my judgment was clouded. I did some foolish things, needlessly putting myself in jeopardy. I had already been eating too much and drinking way too much. Women were easily available after the liberation, and I didn't exercise a lot of self-discipline in that area either. The worst decision I made was my foray into the black market, a game high in risk and intensity that I played not so much for the money as for the thrill. For a couple of years, in Biala Podlaska, then in Katowitz, and later in Munich, I would be up to my hips in illicit transactions, smuggling merchandise, currency, and gold from one end of Europe to the other.

It seemed like everybody was doing it, including the authorities themselves, but that didn't make it any less dangerous. For our first "business trip," Guz, Berensztejn and I decided to return to the Soviet Union to buy gold coins that we would sell for a high price back in Poland. Although we barely escaped with our lives less than a year before, we were ready to tempt fate again.

We came by our initial stake in an odd way. Rumors abounded that a number of Jews, before they fled or were apprehended, had hidden away valuables. One tale concerned a wealthy family that was supposed to have cemented a box of cash inside one of the walls of their house. As far as I know, none of us ever went looking for this "buried treasure," but one day Guz stumbled upon a large bag in one of the closets of our Jewish compound that appeared to contain thousands of diamonds! It seemed too good to be true, and it was. We took the gems to one of the few jewelers left in town and he convinced us that they were made of zircon, a cheap mineral that could be processed to look like diamonds. Nevertheless, we received some cash for the artificial stones and it was enough to get us started.

Our plan was to purchase government-minted five- and ten-ruble gold pieces in the Soviet Union. We would buy them with paper rubles the authorities had introduced as the temporary currency in Biala Podlaska. We knew that so late in the war people in the USSR were desperate and would be willing for a small premium to sell their gold coins for our paper money, which their stores were required to accept. Back in Poland, the gold pieces would be worth much more. As a code word, we referred to the coins as piglets, *chazzermlach* in Yiddish. Other smugglers usually sewed them inside their clothing or even stuck them in a roll up their behinds. Thankfully, we had a better way of bringing the valuable chazzermlach home: special inlays in the soles of our shoes.

We went by train back across Volhynia and then all the way to Kiev, a trip of almost four hundred miles. This time the identification documents we'd received in Rovno were useless. They were

FLIMFLAM MAN | 125

almost a year old by now and in any event we could hardly claim that we were preparing for a mission to parachute into Poland when traveling in the opposite direction. We were draft dodgers and smugglers without proper papers or even train tickets.

So we thought it would be good not to come into contact with the border police. In teams of two or three they manned the railways checking documents from one end of the moving train to the other. And they were always suspicious because forged papers were commonplace. One of us, in a forward position, would try to spot the guards when they entered the car before ours. The lookout would signal the other two and we would all go out the rear door, climb up on the roof, and stay there until we saw them exit. Then we'd come back down and take our seats as if we had every right to be there.

I made three of these trips, one from Biala Podlaska and the other two from Katowitz, a much larger city about two hundred miles to the southwest where I settled next. Berenzstejn was along only for the first one and then left for Italy, from where he would eventually immigrate to America. Sadly, I would not see Max Bernstein, as he was known in the States, for many years. Guz, who was much older than I and should have known better, was my partner on all three of these madcap ventures. And during the last trip we were nearly caught. As usual, we climbed down from the roof as we watched the uniforms enter the next car. But this time, probably because they had forgotten something, they quickly turned around and walked right back toward where we were sitting. We were saved only because they didn't look at the passengers and quickly left. That was it for Guz, however. He said that if I so much as mentioned chazzermlach again he'd break my legs.

Our new base of operations, Katowitz, was close to the Czech border and had a more western orientation. Guz and I lived in that large industrial city for about a year while I set my sights even further west, on Munich, the black market capital of Europe. From Katowitz, I made numerous trips there on my own, carrying in the false bottom of my suitcase German marks that I'd bought in Poland with zlotys. I would use them to buy top-quality German goods that would fetch a high price back in Katowitz. And I would take home more zlotys, too, which I could get for almost nothing in Bavaria, and start the whole process again.

Not wanting to deepen my roots in the land of my birth, I never bothered obtaining a Polish passport, and therefore had the same problem on my journeys to Munich as I had earlier trafficking gold coins in the Soviet Union. Fortunately, I was able to rely on an elderly woman in Prague who arranged for a guide to escort me, and usually a few other illegals, through an unguarded part of the German-Czech border. We would pay her a small fee for making the arrangements as well as allowing us to stay in her house for the several days it took for the guide to arrive. Sometimes we would stop in the town of Pilsen and drink a big mug of beer before continuing by truck up the mountains to the frontier. Then the guide would point to a slope a few hundred yards away and say "That's Germany. It's safe to go now." After hiking for an hour or so we would arrive in Hof, a small town in the northeastern tip of Bavaria. There, I would buy a ticket for the next train to Munich. Neither the guides nor the go-between ever cheated us, and in general I came to like the Czechs. They and their new government in these immediate postwar years were sympathetic to foreign Jews.

My luck as a smuggler finally ran out during my last trip in the fall of 1946. It began in Munich, where another former partisan, Shimmel Greenspan, casually asked if I cared to accompany him on a jaunt to visit his relatives in Budapest, three hundred and fifty miles away. Immediately, I saw a business opportunity in the making and agreed to go along. At the time I was running high-quality leather, as smooth as velvet, from Germany into Poland. It was used to make fancy shoes or handbags, and I was certain the fine skins would be a hit in the sophisticated Hungarian capital.

Our scheme was to pose as Hungarians returning home from Bavaria. We hoped to blend in with the crowd of millions of Europeans whom the Nazis had deported to Germany for forced labor and who were now being repatriated. For me, never having been to Hungary and not knowing the Magyar language, it was a bit of a stretch. But we wrapped our clothes around the leather, put the bundle in the back of Greenspan's truck, a tiny pickup with a canvas top, and off we went. Because gas was scarce, we brought along several bottles of good vodka—exactly the right commodity for bribing Russian soldiers along the way who gladly siphoned fuel from their vehicles into ours.

Everything went well until we rolled into Budapest. With the great city reduced to rubble, and all of the bridges over the Danube destroyed, we had difficulty locating Greenspan's people. We finally parked the truck and walked about half a block to ask for directions. By the time we returned I saw we were in a terrible fix. Soviet military officials had smelled something and were swarming over our things. It didn't take long for them to find the contraband, which they confiscated immediately. Then they arrested us and drove us to the police station for questioning.

Standing before a Red Army officer, Greenspan began with the excuse that what we brought into the country—dozens of square meters of expensive leather—were just gifts for his relatives. The interrogator flew into a rage, and we both saw there was no choice but to reveal everything. We began by telling him who we really were, Polish Jews who had lost our families, fled into the forest, and joined the partisans. And as we talked I soon got the sense—from his features, gestures, and speech patterns—that the Soviet officer was also Jewish and that we were winning his sympathy. This did not mean he was simply going to release us, however. He lectured us for hours, both showing pity and berating us for our stupidity. Our "economic crimes" could result in a sentence of fifteen years at hard labor, he thundered, and the government would like nothing better than to make an example of Jewish profiteers like us. He finally released us and ordered the return of our little vehicle. But to teach us a lesson, he kept the merchandise and our money.

This was a dire warning and it stayed with us about fifteen minutes. As soon as we were back on the street we wanted to make up our large financial loss. Remembering that in Prague there was a shortage of cigarettes, I suggested to Greenspan that we buy about a dozen cases in Budapest and take them across the border into Czechoslovakia. To conceal the cigarettes we bought crates of grapes that made it look like we were farmers on the way to the market. Although the Soviet officials had seized all the cash in our pockets, they hadn't thought to look in the inlays of our shoes where we hid large bills in American dollars for just this type of emergency.

After finally finding Greenspan's family and spending some time with them, we set out on our risky return trip. First we used the grapes to bribe the guards on the Czech border. Once in Prague, we sold the cigarettes, the remaining crates of our camouflage, and even the pickup truck on the black market. After a few days in the familiar safe house there, we entered Bavaria as I had done several times before, illegally crossing the mountainous frontier with the aid of paid escorts. We told ourselves that our Hungarian excursion, which had not turned out the way we planned, didn't end up so badly after all.

I did have one legitimate business in those postwar years, a winery in Katowitz that I operated for six months with Isaac Guz, a fellow named Shmuel Greenberg who had been in the rooming house with us in Biala Podlaska the year before, and two Poles. Like so much else at that time, there was no rhyme or reason to it. I knew nothing of the wine business but was willing to give it a try.

Before the war the winery had been in Jewish hands. Now, in 1945, it was one of many abandoned businesses in Katowitz, a major commercial center. The concern was taken over by two Polish partners: a chemist to oversee the fermentation process and a professional "taster," a guy with an enormous belly who waited forever in silence after he sipped the wine before announcing his verdict. The two Poles probably brought in Greenberg, and later Guz and myself, because they feared that if their "acquisition" were ever investigated it would look better if there were a few Jews in the company. They needn't have worried. The last thing the People's Republic of Poland thought about was making restitution.

Guz and I were there for one complete run and the five of us

From left: Greenberg, Guz, and I at work in the wine business

At left, with friends in Katowitz soon after the war's end

oversaw a big operation. The wine was produced in a cellar a block long with huge, wooden vats along the walls from floor to ceiling. Though we had only one kind of grape, we created an array of six or seven different labels for the exact same wine. As we expected, people said they liked one better than the other.

I found being a vintner exciting, from crushing the grapes to bottling the wine. (A few years later in America, as a new immigrant, I seriously considered buying the nearly defunct Paul Masson Winery near San Jose but didn't have the money.) At the age of twenty-one, I learned the business quickly, relying on others to tell me what I needed to know. This certainly raised my self-esteem. It sure felt better than trying to outwit the border patrol on a smuggling trip.

Katowitz was good to me in other ways. For a Polish city it was relatively tolerant and many survivors chose it as a refuge. There were twenty-five thousand Jews there by 1946—fifteen percent of the total population—and I felt a lot more comfortable than I had in postliberation Biala Podlaska. Guz and I shared a luxury apartment that even had indoor plumbing.

Although Guz, in middle age and with a steady girlfriend, would stay home at night, I was usually out on the town. I also spent a good deal of time in the house of a wealthy Jew named Chaban who, along with his family, had passed as Catholic during the war. He had prospered in textiles before the German invasion and now was one of the kings of the black market. Chaban took a liking to me and offered me both a regular smuggling run to Paris and the possibility of marrying his daughter. I declined both, preferring to focus on my new occupation and remain a bachelor.

But after half a year as a winemaker, even before we had seen any profits, I decided to move on, leaving the apartment to Guz and his girlfriend (who themselves would not remain much longer), and walking away from my twenty percent share in the partnership. Greenberg saw the wine business in Katowitz as his future, but I felt that even if we had recently gotten a lucky break or two, Poland was a dead end. By early 1946, I knew that I had to leave.

But what was the next stop? The mass movement of young Polish Jews heading to Palestine was well under way by now despite the fact that most of them had to enter the Holy Land unlawfully because of Britain's White Paper. In light of all that had happened in the past few years, not least of all the fresh anti-Semitic atrocities committed by Poles against returning survivors, every Jew seemed to be a fervent Zionist.

On numerous occasions along the well-worn smuggling routes, I'd encounter agents sent from Palestine, men in their twenties known as *shlichim*, or emissaries, who tried to convince me to make aliyah. They, too, were seeking gaps in the frontier, reliable mountain guides, and safe houses, but their contraband was young Jews. This was the semisecret organization known as Bricha (meaning "flight" in Hebrew) that in the mid-1940s brought almost a quarter million survivors to Palestine. They promised to make all the arrangements to get me by train to Italy, or somewhere else on the Mediterranean, from where I would sail to the Promised Land. They offered to pay my passage and help me every step of the way. "We need you," they pleaded, "to build a Jewish state, the only valid response to our people's suffering in Europe."

I listened to them with respect but always put them off. Many of my former partisan comrades did immigrate to Palestine, and a few even worked for Bricha. But it wasn't for me. My decision was based on some of the same reasons I refused to join the Red Army after I emerged from the forest in 1944. Call me selfish, if you will, but I wasn't ready to fight in another war, regardless of how noble it was. As the only survivor of my family, my goal was simply to stay alive.

I knew even then that many of the ships to Haifa and Jaffa were intercepted by the British Navy and that the hopeful Jewish emigrants were interned in awful detention camps. I was also aware of the bloody conflict with the Arabs and the prospect of an armed struggle that could last for years. Besides, I was too much of an individualist to live on a kibbutz—which seemed to be the only thing these idealistic, left-wing emissaries ever talked about—and to join with others in a socialist experiment. Business was in my blood, and I wanted to be completely free in making my way in the world.

And though I was not without sympathy for Zionism, there was something else that left a bad taste in my mouth during those early postwar years. Maybe it wasn't fair, but I blamed the Palestinian Jews for their failure to come to the aid of their brothers in

Nazi-occupied Europe. The Jewish nationalists had been so shrill in the late 1930s, sending dynamic speakers like Jabotinsky and Ben-Gurion into Poland to harangue the masses, but they seemed to turn their backs on us as soon as the war broke out—just when we needed them most. If they had sent an emissary *then,* with a clear wake-up call to the Jews in the ghetto, it would have gone a long way toward saying that they had not forgotten about us. Now it bothered me that after I had made it out alive, with no help from them, they would make a big pitch about how much they needed me.

Naturally I thought of Simcha and Sol and how they were the devoted Zionists in our family. If they had survived, one or both of them likely would have made aliyah. But I couldn't live my life based on what they might have wanted for themselves or for me.

As erratic as my movements were then, I can now see that I was gradually headed in a westerly direction, from Rovno, which became part of the Soviet Union, to Biala Podlaska in Poland, and then to Katowitz near the Czech border. My next home was Munich, where I lived for about a year and a half before finally sailing to America in September 1947.

I was in the flood of over a quarter million East European Jews—the high tide would be in mid-1946—that engulfed the British and American zones of occupied Germany. Most were fleeing the persecution of their neighbors and hoping to immigrate to Palestine or the West. In addition to the Jews, there were about a million others who came across the border refusing repatriation. These included Poles, Ukrainians, Hungarians, Balts, and others who had been anticommunists before or during the war and now feared for their safety under the new Stalinist regimes in their homelands. Czechoslovakia, still outside the Soviet orbit,

My postliberation westward journey, 1944–47

was fairly lenient in allowing refugees to cross its frontiers, and for a while the Allied military government in Germany opened the border as well. But even when the gates were closed, a multitude of "infiltrees," as we were called, made it through illegally, usually overwhelming the authorities. With no nation willing to take any significant number of the Displaced Persons permanently, we soon became one of the world's greatest humanitarian problems.

Some eighty percent of the DPs were housed in camps organized by the Allied armies, but like most former partisans I neither needed nor wanted that kind of institution. Having been "on the outside" during the war, I was certainly going to remain on my own now. I rented a private room near the center of Munich.

On the streets there was crime everywhere you looked: prostitution, black market trade in goods and currency, bribery, and plain theft. The city was a bizarre meeting place of Germans trying to cope with defeat, DPs struggling to put their lives back together, and GIs out to have fun. You saw black servicemen with blond fräuleins, American Jewish social workers speaking broken Yiddish to concentration camp survivors, and former high ranking German officials buying coffee, cigarettes, and nylons under the table from foreigners.

The town that had been so central in Hitler's rise to power was suffering badly. Almost half of Munich lay in ruins from bombing attacks, and the walls of the buildings left standing were riddled with holes from shelling. The population was reeling from the strict rationing imposed by the U.S. military government. German women trudged to the main train station every day, carrying pitiful placards with the names and photos of their missing men, hoping that an arriving passenger might provide some information.

The troubles of the "master race" didn't bother me in the least. The nightclubs, beer cellars, and dance halls were full every night and that was what I cared about. Postwar Munich was a wild party held on the corpse of Nazism, and I was one of the revelers.

Even in defeat, the Germans were still infected with the anti-Semitism of the Third Reich. The presence of hundreds of thousands of East European Jewish refugees in their midst hardly made things better. It didn't surprise me to learn later that a survey of public opinion in Bavaria at that time showed that four in ten approved of violent acts against Jews and another four harbored deep anti-Jewish attitudes. But the Germans had been disarmed and were under the tight control of the Allied occupation. They couldn't do much more than sulk.

I was attracted by the business opportunities this place offered and fascinated by the fact that everything was for sale. At the *Boerse,* the raucous, open-air currency market, people speculated in Reichsmarks, military scrip, dollars, and gold coins of every kind. The exchange rate changed minute by minute, and it didn't take me long to figure out that several powerful traders frequently manipulated the market. If they wanted to buy dollars, say, they would first sell some to drive the price down and then suddenly step in and purchase a much larger amount at the artificially depressed level.

The main black market for goods was located on Möhlstrasse, where many DPs illegally sold or bartered some of their excess rations of food, clothing, soap, and tobacco to the needy locals. There was also a lively trade in more expensive items ranging from cigarette cases, to *shtuppers* (slang for elaborate watches with one or more buttons to push), to diamonds. The Munich police constantly raided the black market, arresting countless DPs even on suspicion. And although Jews were only a small minority of the offenders, the German press played up the pettiest infractions to make it appear as if a Yiddish-speaking Mafia had invaded the country.

In fact, all of that was minor compared to the real organized crime rings, predominantly non-Jewish, that stole entire railway cars of American goods intended for the relief organizations that served the camps. As freight came down through Germany from the northern shipyards, thieves would unhook one boxcar here and another there so that by the time it reached its destination in Bavaria what started out as a long train ended up a short one.

Still, more than enough aid arrived, and my occasional visits to friends in the DP camps in the Munich area convinced me that the Jewish survivors (who for everyone's benefit were generally separated from the others,) were being properly cared for. Certainly serious abuses had occurred before I arrived in Munich, and even during my time there I was aware of the restlessness and frustration that, not surprisingly, pervaded the camps. Sometimes fights broke out between the Jews and the German cops, and both

occasionally tangled with American soldiers. Yet overall, my rec-
ollection is of well-dressed, well-fed residents who were gradually regaining their strength. Today, I give a lot credit to the JDC
(American Jewish Joint Distribution Committee) for this. Among
dozens of private relief organizations serving the refugees the Joint
was by far the largest and most effective. The camps fielded sports
teams, published newspapers, and held cultural events. Many of
the DPs already had jobs, and their children attended school. There
were weddings, births, and celebrations of every Jewish holiday.

But I spent most of my leisure hours in town, drawn to the
freewheeling Munich nightlife. People from the most diverse
backgrounds became my beer-drinking buddies instantly. For the
first time in my life I met Americans and found them very friendly. Most just needed Reichsmarks, which I gladly sold them for
their military scrip. But a few others, themselves the children and
grandchildren of East European Jews, were eager to hear how I
survived the war as a partisan.

I had never seen blacks before, but I accepted the African
American GIs as simply another part of the varied backdrop.
Among the Germans looking for a good time, there was a much
higher percentage of young women than men because so many of
their soldiers had been killed or badly wounded, or were still being
held as POWs in the Soviet Union. The bar scene was rounded
out by con men seeking their next victims, Nazi war criminals
planning their escape, communists plotting revolution, and foreign spies gathering intelligence.

A lot of people reinvented themselves in this environment,
posing as something they weren't. In my case, I felt a lot better in
the role of a junior Soviet military attaché than as a Jewish refugee from Poland making his living on the black market. With my
trusty naval officer's coat (a security blanket if there ever was one)

and decent command of the Russian language, my new persona emerged without much effort—especially in the company of an attractive German girl.

Not revealing my real name or address, I entered into liaisons with a couple of these locals. It was both exciting and repulsive to be physically close with the women of the enemy. In a crude way, more like an adolescent than an adult, I felt I was getting back at them with my deception and performing an act of revenge. I wounded them most, I think, by giving them a false sense of hope about their loved ones still in Siberian prison camps. They were desperate for news and I told them that I could find out the whereabouts of a father, an uncle, a husband, a brother, even giving the impression I might be able to intercede on their behalf. A few weeks later, after my fictional "return from the Kremlin," (in actuality I had been smuggling goods to Poland) I dangled a tantalizing piece of "inside information" in front of each of them just to keep the ruse going. This was the form of torture devised by a youth whose mind was still twisted by the demons of hate. But such sordid behavior hardly eased my pain. Looking at the photos of the German soldiers in their shiny uniforms, and even being shown some valuables that had been looted from Jews and shipped home from the eastern front, I forced myself to keep a straight face while my soul was being ripped apart.

Fortunately, I also had a circle of true friends in Munich. That city would eventually be the springboard out of Europe for many people I knew: former members of Maks' unit and civilian camp, some of the survivors I had been with in Biala Podlaska after its liberation, and several Jews I had met in Katowitz. Guz arrived, too. Although he was now a married man with a child, I still saw him often.

In postwar Munich

My girlfriend was Eva Rosenzweig, a few years older than her sister Helenka and older than I. They had very different personalities. Helenka was serious and virtuous. Eva was more passionate, a free spirit willing to travel with me in open boxcars from Munich to Poland usually with some contraband in tow. But like the rest of her family, there was an aristocratic side to her, a combination of refinement and beauty that was especially embodied by her mother. Mrs. Rosenzweig had moved to Lublin after its liberation and with Eva and Helenka I once visited her tastefully furnished home. There, the two sisters taught me the waltz, and I discovered with delight that I had a flair for dancing, a pastime I have enjoyed ever since.

There was another Rosenzweig sister, the eldest of the three, whom I also got to know. She had just separated from her husband and needed a Jewish bill of divorcement, known as a *get*. But we couldn't find a rabbi in Munich willing to issue it, so I accompanied her to another German city to obtain it. We had to wait three days as well as pay a high price. It was not an experience that raised my already low opinion of the Orthodox establishment.

The Rosenzweig family wanted to immigrate to America but as Polish Jews there was little chance in 1947. Australia took them in, however, and all three sisters raised families there. They frequently corresponded with me, not in Yiddish but in an elegant Polish hand, for many years. I would long remain their "*Juzeczek*," or "dearest little Joseph."

It was also in Munich that I met Paul Sade, a forceful man who would be my closest friend for the next half decade and deeply affect my life on two continents. The first time I saw him was in the famous Hofbrauhaus, where he was sort of holding court carrying on two conversations at once, one in Yiddish and the other in Russian, and drinking a beer to wash down a big bar of chocolate. Out of curiosity, I walked over to this nonconformist, introduced myself, and discovered we had a lot in common. Born and raised in a Volhynian village, where his family operated a flour mill, he had lost his parents in the war and survived by hiding in the forest and taking part in some partisan activities. But in temperament Paul was almost my opposite: outgoing, opinionated, and optimistic. Nothing seemed to bother him.

With two uncles in Baltimore, he was among the tiny group of East European Jews allowed an immigrant visa to the United States. Spending a lot of time with Paul, I began to think about America myself. At first, I wasn't all that sure, but Paul sailed in early 1947 and his letters to me were encouraging. Besides, I constantly heard from other refugees, like the Rosenzweigs, about their desire to immigrate to America even if they had to settle for some other destination. It must be the best place, I told myself, if almost everyone is trying to get there. I recalled, too, the stir that was caused back in Biala Podlaska when someone received an article of clothing from a relative in the Golden Land. It was so much more stylish than anything we had locally. On occasion, new Americans returned to our town for a visit, always appearing as if they had done well.

My prospects for getting in, however, were bleak. I lacked family in the States or anyone willing to sponsor me. I had only a modest amount of money, no higher education, and couldn't speak English. But my biggest problem was the damned immigration quota, essentially unchanged since the 1920s. In that decade, to stop the great influx from Eastern and Southern Europe, Congress passed a series of highly restrictive laws. The legislation drastically limited the total number of immigrants and set quotas for each country, which gave an overwhelming advantage to Scandinavia, Ireland, Germany, and above all Britain, and severely penalized the Slavic and Eastern Mediterranean lands. During World War II even these quotas went unfilled. Officials in the State Department erected high "paper walls" in front of prospective immigrants, often rejecting their applications with the snap judgment: "Likely to become a public charge." As a result, only twenty-one thousand refugees entered the United States in the four years following Pearl Harbor. America was a haven, as one writer of the time put it, "almost as inaccessible as Tibet."

After the war, despite the pressure of over a million displaced East Europeans (about a quarter of them Jews), Washington moved very slowly. President Truman was sympathetic to our plight, but Congress blocked his plans. Only in the summer of 1948 would it approve the Displaced Persons Act that granted over the next four years more than four hundred thousand new slots outside the quota system, about a hundred thousand of which would go to Jews. Prior to that, when I was trying to immigrate, the United States admitted only sixty-five hundred from Poland each year, and thirty thousand from all of Eastern Europe. And those meager quotas were for Jews and non-Jews combined.

It was different for Germans. After the war, Germany's large, unfilled immigration quota was an embarrassment to the State Department. As is well known, their scientists were accepted, as well as many ex-Nazis, including a number of war criminals who slipped through the poor screening process and got the chance to start anew in America. But there were relatively few German Jews trying to enter the States after 1945. An important colony that had survived in Shanghai during the war was on its way to California, but it was small in size compared to the vast numbers of displaced East European Jews.

I didn't know all these details while living in Munich in 1946 and 1947. But the main point was clear: If you were a Pole, America didn't want you; if you were a German, you were welcome. It seemed utterly arbitrary and unfair, especially when I visited the DPs and saw survivors of the concentration camps who were now well on the way toward rebuilding their lives. The Germans, who had been responsible for carrying out the greatest crime in world history, had a much better chance of settling in America than they did.

As I pondered my own future I refused to let this obstacle stand in my way. I would change my status from a Polish Jew to a German Jew, I told myself. All it required was a little creativity. Someone informed me of a small Prussian town, Hindenburg, whose municipal building, containing all its inhabitants' birth and naturalization records, had been demolished by the allied bombings. Fifty miles north of Berlin, it was now in the Soviet zone of occupation, an unlikely place for an American official to show up and ask questions. Of course there might exist a national depository for all this data, I thought, but that was a risk I was willing to take.

I prepared a story that was simple and plausible. It was that my father, from Biala Podlaska, had immigrated to Germany in the early 1920s (as many Polish Jews in fact had done) and settled in Hindenburg (which, in reality, was near the well-known Polish Jewish emigre community of Prenzlau) and taken out German citizenship. I was born there in 1924, but, because things didn't work out, the family moved back to Poland when I was still a small child. Perhaps the fact that I now had a regular Munich street address and didn't reside with the other refugees in a crowded camp helped my case as well.

With Hindenburg as my birthplace and Germany as my country of origin, I quickly received notification from the U.S. consulate in Munich that my application had been approved. It hadn't even required an interview so I was never called upon to tell my tall tale. I still had some doubts about immigrating, though, and every few weeks the consulate sent me a card in the mail urging me to come in and pick up the visa. The Americans could not have cared less about my situation as a Polish Jew; as a German Jew I was being courted.

Finally, in the summer of 1947, I decided to make the leap. I told the consular official that I was ready to collect my immigration papers. In the packet I found a steamship ticket, leading me to believe that if you were admitted to the United States, the government provided passage along with the visa. (Later I found out that it was the Joint Distribution Committee that had paid my fare, and in the 1960s, after I felt secure financially, I surprised them with a "reimbursement" check for twenty-five thousand dollars. The executive director traveled to California to thank me personally.)

The ship was to sail from the northern port of Bremerhaven, and I had an emotional farewell as I left my house in Munich for

On my way to America, September, 1947

the train station. My two landladies, a woman of around sixty and her mother who was over eighty, had actually been very protective of me during the year and a half I occupied a spare room in their large, comfortable home. Decent people in every way, they had grown attached to their lodger, whose true background they knew. They were sorry that I was going so far away.

The two women made an important impression on me because I despised almost all the other Germans I encountered in Munich after the war. Whenever I saw a man on the street I asked myself what terrible crimes he had committed against Jews. To me the Nuremberg trials held eighty miles away were a joke because they targeted only the leadership of the Nazi Party and a tiny fraction of those involved in the Final Solution. I wanted the whole German nation to pay for what it had done. Even today, in a setting as benign as a golf course in Marin County, when I hear a Teutonic accent from a man of that generation I have to restrain myself from getting upset.

But that is precisely why the example of my Munich landladies was so vital. Although I never once asked them if they had resisted Hitler, I sensed they had not approved of the Third Reich and never harmed a Jew themselves. Had it been up to people like them, Nazism would not have come to power. Yes, men they loved had gone off to war to fight for an evil enterprise. But these women were kindhearted souls, and I could not consider them guilty along with the rest. Saying *Auf Wiedersehen* to them, I realized that I had seen just about everything during my stay in Munich, including even a couple of "good Germans."

As it turned out, my ship's departure was delayed "indefinitely" and, knowing they hadn't yet rented out my room, I returned, unannounced, to that house. The ladies had been crying a lot since I left, and their eyes were still red when they opened their door to me again.

The wait turned out not to be long and I headed out of Bavaria again, this time for good. I sailed to America on the *Ernie Pyle,* a troop and cargo carrier that had recently been converted to a passenger ship. It was a rough crossing that lasted about two weeks as the boat bobbed up and down on waves over twenty feet high. But luck was with me again as I was among the few passengers who did not get seasick. In fact, I can still recall the excellent food they served on board.

I had plenty of time to think about what lay ahead. I planned to meet Paul in Baltimore, but that would just be the beginning. The real question facing me as I looked out on that endless, churning sea was nothing other than what to do with my life in

The Ernie Pyle, *which brought me to the United States*

the New World. Very soon I resolved to work for myself, to be a businessman, an entrepreneur. If I prized anything it was my independence. Whatever happens, I told myself, I'm going to be my own boss.

Like every immigrant I was eager to catch sight of the Statue of Liberty as my ship entered New York Harbor. We all went up on deck, hours before we were due to dock, but it was late at night and too dark and foggy to see anything until Ellis Island opened and we went through processing the next morning. In the first light of day, what awed me most were the towering buildings of Lower Manhattan visible across the water. Nothing I had ever seen prepared me for those beauties of steel, glass, and concrete. My worldly possessions consisted of eight hundred dollars and a used Leica camera. But I indulged myself in the fantasy that someday I would own one of those skyscrapers.

NINE

Reading the Signs

STEPPING OFF THE FERRY FROM ELLIS ISLAND and setting foot in Manhattan, I saw other immigrants meet with the excited shouts and warm embraces of relatives. Laughter, cries of joy, and prayers of thanksgiving filled the air.

There were forced moments, too, when people at a loss for words felt they had to say *something*: "Oh, Moishe, I got your pictures in the mail and now I can't believe I'm seeing you in person!" Or, "Mendel, they must have fed you well on the boat; you don't look bad at all." Even that sort of greeting would have meant a lot to me, but there was no one waiting for Yosel Epelbaum. Of the hundred and fifty million people in America, I knew only one, Paul Sade, and he was not about to leave his job in Baltimore and come up to New York just to hug me when I came ashore.

Most of those welcomed by friends or family went off with them. The rest of us stood around, a bit sheepishly, until HIAS (the Hebrew Immigrant Aid Society, which took over for the Joint Distribution Committee once we were in the States) arranged for a bus to take us uptown. Our destination was a hotel on Forty-third Street where I was assigned a small room of my own. There, close to Times Square, I would spend about two weeks. It was a thrilling place for a young man who had grown up in a Polish town without electricity and had lived in the woods for a year and a half. Sure, Katowitz and more so Munich were major cities, but they had been wrecked by war. I was now in the middle of something else—a metropolis throbbing with vitality, the center of the universe.

Everyone was moving fast and with great purpose. Shoppers dashed into the crowded stores, theatergoers hurried to get to the shows on time, and commuters rushed in and out of the packed subways. It was all very stimulating.

But with no place to go, I led an aimless existence. I had not come as a tourist with a list of sights to see, and anyway I had no one to show me around. Even more limiting was my lack of English, causing problems as soon as I left the hotel. That's why I ate most of my meals at the Horn & Hardart Automat where what you saw was what you got. You could look through the glass door of a little compartment, put a few coins in a slot, turn the handle, and, wonder of wonders, pull out your food. But at a regular restaurant some advance planning was required to ensure there would be no surprises. Trying hard not to be rude, I would walk through the place and glance around at the other diners until I saw someone eating a dish I thought *I'd* like. Then I would sit at a table nearby so when the waiter came over I could order just by pointing at the other person's plate.

I wasn't completely alone in the big city because my girlfriend Eva Rosenzweig had given me the number of some relatives she had in Brooklyn, a family headed by a widow with two grown daughters, one of them single and the other married. The son-in-law, a lawyer, picked me up in his car and drove me over the bridge to meet everyone for a Shabbes dinner. After the meal, the mother got right to the point: Would I be willing to walk around the block a few times with her unmarried daughter? I agreed, felt awkward in such a contrived situation, and nothing came of it. Later I wondered if Eva had made this connection more for the sake of that family than for me. But it didn't matter. I was a lonely guy, and it was good just to have some home cooking and be with people I could talk to.

There was nothing at all positive about my visit to the Biala Podlaska Society, the *landsmanshaft* of former Bialers living in the New York area. I had obtained their phone number from a distant cousin whom I'd met by chance in Munich, and with so much time on my hands figured that I had nothing to lose by going to see them.

I entered a nondescript office and found about half a dozen older men whose dress and manner indicated to me they had immigrated decades before. They listened while I briefly told them about my family and my service in the partisans. Then they invited me to share some food. But when we finished eating, they all got up and huddled together, talking quietly and leaving me at the table with no idea of what was going on. They returned, said goodbye, and handed me a check from the society for twenty-five dollars.

Deeply hurt, I gave it right back to them. I had not gone there asking for money and in any case they hadn't inquired about my financial needs. They just sized me up, and, before sending me on my way, figured that a handout was the right thing. It felt like they were saying: "This nebbish, let's give him twenty-five dollars."

In a city full of strangers, the society was a link to my hometown. Through its members I might have made contact with other Bialers who had known the Epelbaums. At the very least, I could have discovered a sympathetic *landsman* willing to befriend me and relieve the loneliness I felt. But they treated me with all the compassion of government bureaucrats, and I had no desire to return. They were so high-handed in dispensing what I *didn't* need, that I could not bear to ask them for what I truly lacked.

Their behavior was typical of the arrogance and insensitivity I encountered from many American Jews in these postwar years. Especially those who had been immigrants themselves tended to look down their noses at newcomers. Someone who had grown up in a Lower East Side tenement early in the century and now lived in a modern apartment building in the Bronx or a row house in Brooklyn enjoyed a wicked delight in referring to us recent arrivals exactly the way they themselves had once been branded—"greenhorns." How I hated that ugly word. And how unfair it was when applied to Holocaust survivors. I understood that green meant a kind of raw immaturity, but even though I was only twenty-three I felt I had been through a lot more than these smug city dwellers. And why "horn"? Did we stick out that much that it appeared we had sprouted an animal-like body part? Thankfully, you rarely hear the term greenhorn today in connection with the wave of Jewish immigrants that has arrived in recent decades from the former Soviet Union.

I know that newcomers from every part of the world and in every era have been met with haughty, stuck-up attitudes by their own countrymen who preceded them. I suppose that's human nature. If you can point to someone else as a bumbling foreigner it must mean that you yourself fit in perfectly.

But we survivors were met with a coldness that went even deeper. Reflecting on the initial conversations I had in the States, I realize now how superficial those exchanges were. "Oh, you survived as a fighter in the forest, but your parents, brothers, and sister didn't make it. I see." And then it was on to a new subject. Maybe they behaved that way out of guilt for not having pressured the Roosevelt administration to rescue us. Or perhaps it was like the uneasiness of a person paying his condolences at a funeral who doesn't know what to say to the immediate family members of the deceased. It may even have been that they wanted to spare themselves the pain of finding out the whole grisly truth of what had so recently happened across the ocean. Whatever the reason, we were snubbed as immigrants and shunned as survivors. This would all change, but in 1947, when I needed it most, I cannot say that American Jewry extended a heartfelt welcome.

Yet I was anything but depressed as I moved through the bustling midtown streets near my hotel. It was a time of being in limbo and yet one of intense anticipation because I had the feeling that after a short period of waiting I would get a fast start in the Golden Land. Through the windows of delicatessens I saw cooks, and I knew I could be one. I saw grocers and butchers and I thought I could do that kind of work, too. And then I'd move up the ladder from there. I'm a quick study, I told myself. I'll learn on the job and perform as well as the Americans themselves.

My hope was that Paul and I would seek our fortune together. His uncles had given him work in their big dry cleaning establishment in Baltimore, and that's where I went to visit him after coming down on the train from New York. The place was so steamy it took a while to spot him. Paul was in the back of the hot, noisy factory, pressing pants with an industrial-strength iron. He told me to wait for him until his shift ended, in the comfortable home of one of his uncles where he occupied the guestroom. When he returned that evening we began a serious discussion about the future.

First, I asked him how much he was getting paid. "Seventy-five cents," he answered. "This is why you came to America," I said, "to press pants for seventy-five cents an hour?" It didn't take him long to realize that he could do a lot better. After talking it over for a couple of days we decided to hit the road, head west, and see what opportunities were out there. I was more than ready to end my stay in New York. And, besides, HIAS, preparing for an even larger wave of immigrants, was encouraging us to relocate elsewhere. So we went back to Manhattan long enough to pick up some belongings I'd left behind and then boarded a train for Chicago.

I don't remember putting a lot of thought into our destination. It was a city known for commerce and seemed to be the most logical next step. "New York, Chicago" had the right ring to it. But about two or three days after we arrived there and rented a cheap room near the Loop, the weather turned raw. It was still October, but the wind blowing off the lake was so strong it almost carried us down the street. You didn't have to walk in that town, you were tossed around by the elements. As an icy blast virtually blew us past the Greyhound bus station I noticed a large, inviting poster in the window beckoning people to San Francisco. It featured, of course, a magnificent bird's-eye photo of the Golden Gate Bridge, an engineering marvel I had read about in the newspapers back in Biala Podlaska in the late thirties. It's the longest suspension bridge in the world, I informed Paul, as we steadied ourselves on the sidewalk. I would sure like to see it, I said.

They also enjoy a mild and sunny climate out there, we told each other. In fact, I had heard a lot about California in just the short time I'd been in the States. Everyone, it seemed, from established American Jews to recently arrived refugees, wanted to move there. But people usually had something holding them in the

East—a job, friends, or family. Neither Paul nor I, though, had anything to lose. So, without any hesitation, we went in, walked up to the counter, and bought two one-way tickets on a bus leaving the next day. It wasn't that different than my decision to cross the Atlantic: In Europe, America was everybody's first choice and in America the best place appeared to be California.

It took four days and three nights to get to San Francisco, the longest trip across land that I had taken in my life. I could hardly believe that after going so far in one direction, I remained in the same country. I covered more ground than if I had traveled from Russia to Spain.

Everything impressed me, not least of all the large and powerful motor coach itself. We traveled over broad new highways and on back roads, too. And all along the route people kept getting on and off so I got to see a cross section of the populace as well as the astonishingly vast landscape. There were farmers, factory workers, and soldiers sitting near us; there were blacks, Hispanics, and American Indians. I know of some European immigrants who remained for many years in New York City before venturing west of the Hudson. I was in the country less than a month and, because I was young and unattached, already taking a coast-to-coast trip.

Paul, always a lively conversationalist, made many new friends on the bus and flirted with a few of the single women who came aboard. At night, trading on his good looks and charm, he would steer one of them to the empty seats in the back and try to fool around a little in the darkness.

Meanwhile, I was trying to pick up some English. In addition to my two mother tongues, Yiddish and Polish, I had acquired Ukrainian, Russian, and German just by hearing them spoken or perusing a newspaper in the language. I had never taken a course or studied a grammar book. That's the way I wanted to learn English. Paul gave me his own suggestion for immersion in the foreign words and phrases: Look out the window and read the signs.

I took his advice and was soon baffled. It appeared that most of the property in the American West was owned by one man named Motel. I saw this sign everywhere and thought it was pronounced "*Muh*tel," the same as a cousin of mine back in Poland. I asked Paul how this guy (evidently an East European Jew) accumulated so many buildings. He looked at me as if I were a child and, after setting me straight, repeated his recommendation: "Just keep reading the signs."

Our long ride finally ended at the Greyhound station at Seventh and Market. It was a bright day, and I liked San Francisco the minute I stepped off the bus. The fresh ocean air, the hilly setting (in those days you could look up Market Street and clearly see Twin Peaks), and the friendly, easygoing pace all appealed to me. Even before we got a room and showered, we decided we needed haircuts and went to a barber a block away from the bus station. Sure enough he was a Jew and invited us home for dinner that evening. In his modest house, he and his wife seemed unaffected by the terrible events of the past decade that still gripped Paul and me. They spoke of vacations, sports, and movies. But this American-born couple was genuinely hospitable to survivors in a way that we had not encountered back east and it made a deep impression on us. We both felt that this was the town where we would settle down.

Within a few days we signed a lease for a small, low-rent apartment on Hayes Street in the middle of the city. Although it was in an old building on a run-down block, we could not have been more upbeat about our prospects. We were excited about remak-

ing ourselves here—not unusual, of course, for free-spirited youths
who since the days of the Gold Rush have been drawn to San
Francisco. But given everything Paul and I had been through, we
were probably among the most exhilarated, and certainly among
the most grateful, of any of the young people who ever made that
journey to the Bay. We had arrived on a Greyhound bus from
Chicago, yet our odyssey began in the inferno of Volhynia even
before we had met one another. It had taken not four days, but
almost four years for the westward wandering to be over. Fate, we
told each other, had plucked us out of the worst place in the world
and deposited us in the best.

Paul and I were as close as brothers by then, bonded by our East
European past, by the trip to California, and by our joint hopes for
the future. We not only shared a bedroom, but also slept in the
same bed. Later we bought a used car together, a 1941 Pontiac, and
shared that, too. I yelled at him every time he brought it back with

In San Francisco in 1948 with the 1941 Pontiac I shared with Paul

a banged-up fender. In San Francisco today, people would think two guys living that way were gay. Well, we were both heterosexuals but we were a couple nonetheless. He was the talker, and I was the listener; he was the aggressive one, and I was the reserved one; he was thick-skinned, and I was sometimes too sensitive.

And I was the one who usually made our dinner when we ate at home. Paul liked my cooking a lot and after I prepared a meal of stuffed duck (using my mother's kishka recipe for the stuffing) he got the idea for the most important thing we would share, a business. He insisted we open a restaurant, and every time we would look at an eatery that was for sale he envisioned me as the chef. But I had no desire to work over a hot grill all day and I wasn't about to let him plan my life.

We debated the issue endlessly. In the meantime we both needed temporary work to meet our living expenses and set aside a little extra toward the day when we would become our own bosses. Paul found a job as a busboy on Van Ness Avenue, in one of the many Foster's cafeterias in town, and quickly worked his way up to cashier. Because of my limited knowledge of English, I turned to the Fillmore, a section of town where Yiddish was heard frequently. This was a residential and commercial district consisting of old Victorian buildings that had survived the earthquake and fire of 1906. In the 1920s and 1930s the neighborhood became a lively entertainment center filled with theaters and restaurants, but it was now in decline. After the attack on Pearl Harbor, the government had ordered the Japanese residents to vacate their homes and spend the war years in remote detention camps. Even earlier many of the upwardly mobile Jewish families had left the area, drawn to better neighborhoods. African Americans from the rural South, drawn to the Bay Area by the booming defense industry, often took their places. But after 1945 that community was ravaged by unemployment, and crime in the area increased.

A large pocket of Orthodox Jews remained, however, and I was hired for two days a week to work in a kosher butcher shop on Webster and McAllister—my first job in America. With the shochet's wife running a grocery store next door, it was a traditional mom-and-pop operation that brought back memories of my family's business in Biala Podlaska. The boss was impressed with my skills as a meat cutter, and on my recommendation he offered a position to another immigrant within a few months— my good friend Isaac Guz. He and his family had received visas to immigrate to America and I wrote urging him to settle in San Francisco. Several years earlier we had fought side by side in the swampy forests near Manievich. Now we were elbow to elbow trimming meat on Webster Street.

Soon I added a second part-time job working late afternoons in a long, narrow diner with a big soda fountain on Sutter Street. My assignment was to cut up fruits and vegetables for salads. I earned only a few dollars for my three hours of labor each day, but they paid me in coins—maybe they thought it would seem more to me that way—and I felt proud walking around with lots of silver jingling in my pockets. I now had more than enough money to patronize the many European-style food shops in the Fillmore, especially old-fashioned bakeries like the Ukraine on Webster Street, known for its authentic pumpernickel.

Early one evening, while Paul and I were waiting for the bus home on the corner of Fillmore and McAllister, a gorgeous blond, a bit older than I, overheard our conversation in Polish sprinkled with Yiddish. She asked where we were from, and I answered Poland. She pressed me further: "Where in Poland?" When I said Biala Podlaska, she seized me by the arm and, without a word, with Paul trailing behind, marched us two shleppers in old European clothes up the block and through the door of a liquor store. I was dumbfounded. What, I wondered, does she want to do with us?

Once inside she exclaimed to the man behind the counter, "Daddy, Daddy, you won't believe this!" He was not only from from Biala Podlaska, but when he found out my name he nearly fainted. He told me that he had gone to heder, the Jewish school for small boys, with my father!

This liquor store owner, whom I always called Mr. Galante, had luckily immigrated to America in the 1930s with his wife and two children, Chaim and Sala. When she discovered me on the street corner, Sala was married to a leading clothing manufacturer about ten years her senior. But she would soon divorce Irving Lipschultz and wed Philip Burton, the vigorous liberal politician destined to serve ten terms in Congress beginning in 1965. When he died suddenly of an aneurysm, Sala easily won election as his successor. Within four years, in 1987, she, too, died in office. During her public life—and she had a high profile even as a congressional wife—she spoke proudly of her Jewish heritage and attributed her burning desire to help the disadvantaged to the persecution her family had suffered in Poland.

I had more to do with her parents, though, than with Sala, already a busy mother in 1948. Mr. Galante, it turned out, needed a "night man" at the liquor store and hired me at once. I was now a kosher butcher in the morning, a salad maker in the afternoon, and a seller of spirits in the evening. Sometimes Galante asked me to open his place, too, at 9 A.M. The shop, located between Turk and Golden Gate, was on one of Fillmore Street's roughest stretches, known as Muscatel Drive by the locals. I had to deal with many drunks. Some of them, after guzzling tequila all night, were so far gone that I found them waiting for me to unlock the door the next morning; they wanted a bottle of IW Harper whiskey to "sober up." Although I worked alone and without a weapon, I felt little danger. It was still rare for a liquor store employee to be shot by robbers in those days.

In any event, Galante was close by. He lived above the store and went up for dinner when I arrived for my six to midnight shift. I didn't know much about the product line but fortunately most of my customers were more than willing to point at what they wanted. They already knew exactly where it was on the shelves. I was starting to speak English by then, but some of the slang eluded me. I recall one guy impatiently repeating, "Gimme a mickey," something that made absolutely no sense until I called up to Mr. Galante and he explained in Yiddish that it meant a small flask of liquor made to fit into a coat pocket.

I saw even more of Mrs. Galante. Like her husband a native of Biala Podlaska who had known my parents, she came to regard me almost like a son. In fact she actually expressed the desire to adopt me, even though I was no longer a minor and felt much older than my twenty-four years. On weekends I usually accompanied her as she shopped and ran errands. The two of us spoke often about my long-term plans. She was proud of her son, Chaim, who owned his own liquor store on Hayes Street, near where Paul and I were living. She wanted me to succeed as well.

Over time the Galantes had acquired a few small pieces of income property that she managed. When something needed fixing, she would bring me over to look at it before calling a licensed repairman. Frequently I got lucky. A kick here or an adjustment there, a screw tightened or a new part added and the problem would be solved. Before long she considered me her handyman, and sometimes I wondered if my usefulness explained some of her affection. Like countless immigrants before and since, I was a source of cheap labor and therefore almost indispensable.

Working for Mrs. Galante was my fourth job. Yet I still had plenty of youthful energy left over. This I devoted to the task that made everything else seem minor in comparison—finding a small business to buy.

Every spare moment we had, Paul and I would scour the newspapers for business opportunities, always responding to promising ads. The right thing finally came along in the fall of 1948, only a year after we had gotten off the bus at Seventh and Market.

We quit all of our jobs and bet everything on an ice cream store named Shirley's, a medium-sized shop on the corner of Forty-fourth Avenue and Judah Street. It was in the fast-growing outer Sunset District, then a working-class neighborhood of recently built attached houses popular with both war veterans and European refugees. Despite the cool and foggy weather at this far end of San Francisco, Shirley's seemed well located. It was on an active commercial thoroughfare with a streetcar line, and close to several schools, the beach, and Golden Gate Park.

Before we bought it we observed a brisk business, not only carefully watching the volume of foot traffic at all hours, but also sneaking a peek at the daily deliveries of cream. The fifty gallons that the owner received every morning were evidence that he had to be making at least twice that much ice cream a day, strongly supporting the sales figures he showed us. The seller, an American named Jim, said he'd take seventy-five hundred dollars for the place, a fair price in our opinion. I was able to scrape up twelve hundred and twenty-five dollars consisting of a thousand in cash—my part-time jobs had enabled me to add two hundred to the stake I had brought into the country the year before—and two hundred and twenty-five from the sale of my Leica. Paul had a bit more than that so together we were good for three thousand dollars.

For the balance we sought a bank loan. We didn't have formal résumés but prepared a hand-written summary of our employment histories during the brief time we had been on the West Coast. Although we lacked an elaborate business plan, we assembled a solid set of calculations based on our thorough study of Shirley's.

Then we confidently walked into a Bank of America branch on Geary Boulevard, sat down with the loan officer, and laid out our case. The banker, a California-born middle-aged man, saw two young foreigners, poorly capitalized and both years away from becoming citizens. But he also sensed that we were honest, able people with the capacity for hard work. It had to count for a lot, too, that we were willing to make a down payment of forty percent, even if that was every penny we had.

The next day we got the loan. It was my first experience with a banker, and I was amazed at how smoothly it went. I didn't need a relative or anyone else to vouch for me. I wasn't held back by being an immigrant or a Jew. Later I learned that we also could have obtained financing from the Hebrew Free Loan Association, which made *non-interest-bearing* loans to entrepreneurs just like us who were going into business for the first time. But even if I had known about it, I would not have been inclined to approach a Jewish organization for help. Nor could I see myself going around to others, asking them to be guarantors, which the HFLA required. There would have been absolutely nothing wrong with that, but it conflicted with the keen sense of independence I felt. I wanted to deal with a commercial bank on my own merits and stand on my own two feet from the very beginning.

We lost no time in signing the papers and closing the deal with Jim. Late the same night we came by the store to get the keys, and he said he would meet us in the morning before the place opened at eleven in order to begin teaching us the trade.

When we negotiated the sale, he promised us a two-week training period to show us how to order the ingredients, operate the appliances, and sell the product. Above all, we were going to learn how to make the ice cream.

But when we arrived at the store—our first day as the new owners—he was nowhere to be found. We'd never thought of getting his home phone number and therefore had no way of contacting him. We didn't even know where he lived. In fact, we were never to see him again, and I doubt he remained in town once he got his money.

So there we were, on our own, the clock showing only a few minutes left before the first customer would walk through the door. It was like a bad dream, finding yourself in someone else's kitchen, not knowing where anything is, and required to serve up desserts for hundreds of people who would be arriving non-stop during the next twelve hours.

We were not the type to panic, however. After fumbling around for a while, we found the ice cream recipes in a box of index cards containing the instructions for each flavor. And then we went to work. It might not have been the greatest ice cream in the world on that first day, but we got no complaints. And soon we really got the hang of it; some people told us that it was *better* than the way Jim was making it.

Within a week we were visited by a salesman from the company providing us with the ingredients for some of our more exotic flavors. Showing off my newly acquired skill as an ice cream maker I had him first taste the vanilla, then the walnut, and finally the tutti-frutti. He was clearly impressed. But I didn't want him to leave without knowing that I was an expert at sherbet as well. The only problem was that in my haste to make up the batch I had forgotten to put in the citric acid—essential in counteracting the

Paul and I in front of Shirley's

sugar and bringing out the fruit's tangy flavor. The guy gulped a big bite and then spat it out on the floor. "It's all sugar," he said with disgust.

Although this was humbling, I quickly put the incident behind me and continued to work on my technique. I also tried to understand the psychology of the consumer. He likes to lick the cone as soon as it's in his hand but then he wants to *find something inside*. Almond ice cream, say, with just three almonds doesn't satisfy him; but with seven of them in the cone, he has something to chew with almost every mouthful. The same with walnuts, marshmallows, cherries. And it was actually cheaper to make the ice cream that way—with generous portions of nuts, fruit, or candy—because those items took up space that otherwise would be filled with cream, the most expensive thing of all. Bananas, for example, was one of our most popular ingredients, and we bought them from a nearby grocer for almost nothing since their skins

Our business card for Shirley's catering department

had already begun to turn black. We soon learned that in their ice cream customers loved the oversweet taste of fruit that normally they would consider too ripe to buy in the market.

We also experimented with the level of butterfat in the cream. In those days before America became so diet-conscious, we felt no compunction about making it richer and richer. In fact, that's how we kept ahead of the competition. Further down Judah near Twenty-third Avenue two guys ran a tremendous ice cream business called Hoo's out of their garage. After doing some detective work we found out the reason for their success: instead of the standard ten percent butterfat, they were using twelve percent. So to outdo them we went to fourteen. We also spied on Herbert's Sherbet on Lombard Street, Garrett's popular creamery on Alemany Boulevard, and just about every other frozen dessert maker in the western part of the city.

But all of this "industrial espionage" was little more than a break from the long workdays we put in at the store, open seven days a week from eleven in the morning to eleven at night. Adding the time needed to set everything up before the customers arrived, and to close up in the evening, it was a fourteen-hour stint. It was so exhausting that we usually alternated: When one of us was at Shirley's, the other would be resting, seeing friends, or driving around to check on our rivals. But that meant whoever was in the store would be alone and have to take his meals while working. My dinner would usually consist of chicken that I'd cook on a hotplate in the back. Between bites I would have to scoop out someone's order. The patrons were friendly—the cold, sweet stuff seemed to put people in a good mood, I noticed—but it was hard to engage them in conversation; I was much too busy and not yet fluent in English. They were naturally curious about who I was and where I had come from. But all I could utter was the word "Yes" to whatever was asked, even to the question of whether I was Greek. Some of them must have thought I was pretty mixed-up.

It was worth the effort, though, to see our business grow to the point where people waited in long lines during the peak evening hours. After a while, one of the customers suggested that, since we had a counter with some seats, we go after the lunch crowd by selling chili that could be finished with ice cream for dessert. I had never even heard of chili. But I got a good recipe, took some five-gallon steel cans home from the store, bought huge quantities of tomatoes, beans, ground beef, and hot peppers, and for days cooked up a storm on the little stovetop in our kitchen on Hayes Street. When it was done, we loaded the massive and unwieldy supply of chili into the backseat of our Pontiac and hauled it out to the Sunset. Of course this meant going up some steep hills. I drove slowly while Paul held the heavy cans steady lest they topple over and ruin everything. It was a mad scene that could have come out of one of the Dean Martin and Jerry Lewis movies that were popular at the time. Had the Department of Health known what we were doing, it would have had a fit. But the chili proved to be a hit, adding another feather in Shirley's cap.

Eda when we were dating

One young woman who came into Shirley's was Eda Kuflik, herself an orphaned survivor but one much more Americanized than Paul or I. She had lived in Northern California since 1941, having immigrated as a young girl with her sister from a children's home in France. I had heard about her from a friend who said Eda and I would make a good couple. And now here she was in person. I was attracted by her flair and wit and fascinated by her high-pitched, girlish laugh, like none I had ever heard before.

One damp night she showed up just before 11. I put the "closed" sign in the window and turned on the jukebox. Forgetting my fatigue, I took her by the hand, led her onto the tile floor of the ice cream store and pretended it was a downtown ballroom. For almost an hour we swung to the lively sound of the big bands.

I think Eda liked my dancing before she liked me. She took me to my first Chinese restaurant, Kwan's on Geary, where a marvelous meal cost fifty cents. She then introduced me to other attractions in "The City" she knew so well. It would take more than four years for each of us to be sure, and during that time we dated other people. But Eda was the one I would marry.

TEN

Becoming Joe Pell

ONCE WE GOT SHIRLEY'S HUMMING, Paul and I moved out of our cramped quarters on Hayes Street into a nicer apartment on Sloat Boulevard much closer to the store. We even had rooms overlooking the ocean. But though we lived and worked in the furthest reaches of the Sunset, on the western edge of the city, we never felt isolated. We explored the whole Bay Area like kids in a candy store and made time for a lively social life.

Every other Sunday night I would drive over to the dance held at the Jewish Community Center, a rambling, Mission-style building on California Street. In those postwar years it was the largest and most vibrant Jewish institution in town, and the live bands it presented drew hundreds of young people from all over.

Virtually everyone there was Jewish. But when you entered the big gym the first thing you noticed was a clear-cut division between the Americans and the recent immigrants. The left side was for the "greenhorns," just as we were called back east. The native-born and those who had arrived in the States more than a decade earlier as children occupied the right side. There was some intermingling between the two camps—our girls certainly glanced over at the other side a great deal—but by and large the youths in each group stuck to their own kind. There was a third contingent as well, the (mostly German) Jews who had come through the Golden Gate after a prolonged stay in Shanghai. Most of them had not been in the death camps and had immigrated with their families. They were therefore more "whole" than we were and more westernized and sophisticated as well. They tended to roam around the dance floor and were socially acceptable to both of the main groups.

Today I have friends who were on the right side of that room over fifty years ago and barely acknowledged my existence. We all laugh about such slights now, but at the time it was no small matter. You had to know your place, and it was obvious where you belonged as soon as you opened your mouth.

Even among those of us on the left side of the gym, interactions could be stilted. To the question, "Where are you from?" many new immigrants answered with a non-specific "Europe," which for a moment allowed for some mystery and held out the possibility of a classy place like Nice or Florence. Of course, almost all of us on the left were from Eastern Europe, and when that came out we'd compare notes a bit on our wartime and post-liberation experiences. By coincidence I met a few people at those dances who had come over on the same ship as me, although I hadn't known them on board. Yet these exchanges did not last long. Very quickly a girl wanted to know what kind of car you owned and what you did for a living. Growing weary of this sort of interrogation, I sometimes said that I was a psychiatrist. That usually stopped the conversation cold, which was my intention. I felt much more at ease at these events as a dancer than a talker.

Another one of my haunts was the Emanu-El Residence Club on Page Street in the Fillmore, an elegant brick structure that leading members of the city's most prestigious temple had built in the early 1920s to house single, working Jewish women. Now it had some survivors along with American-born women from the East and the Midwest. Men were not allowed above the first floor so a "gentleman caller," after being formally announced, had to wait in a reception area for the girl to come down from her room. In this lounge I watched television for the first time. I must have arrived early one evening or been kept waiting a while because I got to see a number of long, elaborate sketches performed by Bob Hope. I couldn't comprehend every nuance of his routine, but I grasped enough of it to laugh my head off. It was my first taste of American mass culture.

But I still had some Old World ways. The only sport that interested me was soccer, which I would play on weekends in Golden Gate Park with other foreigners. And Paul and I were part of a circle of friends, mostly married couples a few years older than we were, that consisted almost exclusively of survivors. Members of this set lived in different parts of the Bay Area, and, once Paul and I felt comfortable leaving someone else in charge of the store for a day, we'd drive over to one of their homes for a big feast made livelier by plenty of vodka. One member of the group, Don Felson, later of Hayward, would remain a lifelong friend. He and his brother Stan had both been partisans in Belorussia and though their brigade was smaller than mine, there were a number of similarities in our wartime activities.

Most of the others in our clique had been in concentration camps, though one of them, Henry Krueger, had escaped and later passed as a non-Jew. With Paul Dab, who had been in Buchenwald, he started a variety store in San Francisco. Paul Fox and his wife, Bella, were survivors who lived for a while in Petaluma, where they worked as chicken ranchers, and sometimes we gathered up there. His brother and sister-in-law, Henry and Minna, lived much closer to us in the Sunset District. Minna's sister, Gutta, had quite a story. She had been liberated from a death camp by a soldier in the British Army and ended up marrying him. A Christian, he converted to Judaism, which required him to undergo circumcision.

Paul Sade and I usually showed up together at these house parties without dates, and the married folks made us the butt of some good-natured jokes. They even had a name for us as a twosome: "Shaker and Shlimazel." While the latter is loosely translated as "unlucky sad sack," I'm not sure to this day of the meaning of the former, although it may come from the English expression "mover and shaker." Which of us was supposed to be "Shaker" and which "Shlimazel" remains a mystery.

These shindigs were a lot of fun. They also served as a way for heavily burdened people to reduce some of the stress they felt as immigrants and survivors. Here, they could chat in Yiddish or Polish without fear of reproach. Here, unlike their encounters with American Jews, much less non-Jews, they had a receptive audience when they recounted what had happened to them during the war.

I needed this outlet, too, I suppose. But I also saw a drawback in remaining bound up with the survivor community. On the East Coast it was common for Holocaust victims to stick together to the exclusion of everyone else. They felt comfortable only in a Yiddish-speaking environment, remaining full of bitterness and mistrusting all non-Jews. Our Bay Area group was nowhere as parochial as that, but it was still too inbred for me. I would have preferred smaller doses of the food, the language, and even the gallows humor of the shtetl that were so prevalent at these get-togethers. Perhaps because I had not been in a concentration camp but rather in the partisans, and in a brigade of mixed nationalities at that, I did not feel so insecure as to cling to other survivors after the war. Nor did I want my life to revolve around a synagogue or any other Jewish organization. My focus was rather on the continental nation that I had crossed by bus and that had already rewarded me amply.

For this reason I had no qualms about changing my name as soon as I was naturalized in 1952. People were always misspelling Epelbaum, assuming it started with an "A," and often they couldn't find it in the phone book. But beyond the inconvenience, the truth is that I didn't want such a Jewish-sounding last name. I had not personally experienced anti-Semitism in San Francisco, but in the aftermath of the Holocaust and in the midst of the Cold War, being so identifiably Jewish made me a little anxious. On top of that, the mass media seemed to encourage conformity in the 1950s. There was little of the open celebration of diversity that we have come to see in recent decades. In Eisenhower's America the ideal citizen didn't wear ethnic or religious distinctiveness on his sleeve.

So when I learned that sometimes even native-born folks took a new name when they moved to California and that it was a simple procedure, I resolved to do it, too. I dropped the "e" and the "baum," leaving "pel." Adding another "l" almost put my ancestors on the *Mayflower*. Indeed, more than a third of a century later, Eda and I were in the audience when our daughter Debra introduced Senator Claiborne Pell of Rhode Island as the featured speaker for the Bay Area's commemoration of the fiftieth anniversary of *Kristallnacht*. We were slightly embarrassed to be put in the spotlight when she proudly noted that whereas he could trace his genealogy back to colonial New England, there were other remarkable Pells whose family tree in America wasn't as deeply rooted.

When I changed my name, Mrs. Galante was furious, a reaction that seemed odd to me at the time. But over the years I have had my own regrets about it and would not object if one of my children went back to Epelbaum. My taking a new name half a century ago was something that made sense when this country was a very different place than it is today. The irony is that America turned out to be an even *more* welcoming land than I thought. I really didn't have to change my name to fit in.

But becoming Joe Pell had to do with much more than what I called myself. The new name was only one part of a larger process. Like every immigrant I made personal choices every day about what to keep and what to discard of the foreign baggage I was carrying. And my adaptation, my acculturation as sociologists would say, was more rapid and thorough than most. It was my nature to change direction in a new environment. I never forgot where I came from. But where I was going would be someplace else entirely.

Such flexibility also affected my ideas about making a living. Here, too, I parted company with many of the other survivors. Typically, they were striving to establish a small business—a five and dime, a liquor store, a grocery, even a poultry farm—and to make it viable required a total commitment, often from both husband and wife.

Paul and I admired them for their perseverance, and we were doing much the same thing ourselves. But there was an essential difference. As hard as we worked in the ice cream shop, we never regarded it as anything more than a steppingstone. We always thought about what would come next. Shirley's felt confining after the initial excitement wore off, and we didn't intend to spend the years ahead penned in by the four walls of a store. Being young and unattached meant that we could assume risks the others couldn't or wouldn't. We wanted to roll the dice. Maybe we would land in a bigger and more stimulating arena.

Even the Galantes, I thought, (for I was unable then to foresee Sala's later accomplishments) seemed satisfied with relatively little. They had been in the city for well over a decade but had they really taken advantage of the opportunity America offered? Mrs. Galante was so cautious that she even tried to dissuade me from buying Shirley's. She thought the postwar years would bring an economic downturn and that it was the worst time to go into a new business. Her son, Chaim, raised and educated in San Francisco, now passed the day like his father, in a liquor store waiting for someone to walk in and buy a pint of whiskey. He was far from poor and earned enough to support a family and buy some good clothes, including a collection of hundreds of neckties. But to his mother's surprise, I didn't envy him in the slightest.

Yet none of this is to say that I did such a great job in planning my own future. Yes I aimed high and would achieve financial success fairly quickly, but probably the best move I could have made in the late 1940s would have been to go to school, at least part-time. I could have learned English better and gotten a basic education. My failure to do so was the biggest mistake of my life, and not a day has gone by since that I haven't been troubled by it. If my goal was to accommodate to America, I left a major obstacle in my path.

It might have been different had I found a true mentor in San Francisco—someone a bit wiser than Mrs. Galante, caring though she was—who could have picked me up by the ears and put me on the right track. Left to my own devices I focused all of my energies on the world of business. A major opportunity was about to emerge.

Early one morning Paul and I, always restless and on the lookout for new ventures, read in the Sunday *Chronicle* that based on the 1950 census, Richmond, across the bay, was the fastest-growing city in California. Swollen by the massive influx of workers needed for new shipyards, its population had quadrupled in the past decade to a hundred thousand.

We decided to shift our attention there with the idea of opening a larger ice cream store modeled on Garrett's operation in San Francisco, a thriving enterprise that we scrutinized from every angle. Garrett (whose ill-fated son Wayne would later become a popular local radio talk show host and dealer in sports memorabilia before taking his own life) made ice cream very high in butterfat. A half-gallon weighed three pounds. And he sold it by weight in a distinctive carton with sloping sides resembling a cottage cheese container.

People felt they got their money's worth, and there was always a crowd in front of his place. Another key to Garrett's success, we concluded, was his location on busy Alemany Boulevard, thousands of cars passing it every day.

Trying to replicate this in Richmond, we found a big lot that was not only on the main drag, MacDonald Avenue, but also faced a park across the street. We tracked down the owner, a Berkeley businessman who was willing to sell, and paid his price without hesitation, convinced this was the ideal site. To put together the needed capital, we put Shirley's on the block and sold it for a nice profit, ironically to a couple living in Richmond. It had supported us well for several years, but now we were on to something with much more potential.

We immediately ran into trouble, however, building the new store. Because of the Korean War, the National Production

Authority limited all private construction projects to five thousand dollars. It was a sum far too low to create what we had in mind and for a while it looked like we would have to defer our dream for the duration.

But we refused to take no for an answer. We applied for a permit that we used mostly to purchase the materials, and because there was no limit imposed on the owner's labor, Paul and I hit upon the solution of essentially building the thing with our own hands. We hired a crew to pour the concrete foundation and put in a stone floor, and bricklayers to erect most of the walls. But the two of us put up the rest of the four-thousand-square-foot structure including the roof, ceiling, and interior woodwork. We didn't even have power tools for the lumber we cut. We used handsaws that we sharpened with a file.

Then Paul began painting the place—and we got into a terrific argument. He insisted on a deep green for the exterior, a sickening choice, I thought, for a creamery. But no matter how strongly I objected, he kept slapping that awful color on the walls. I realized then that we would not be partners forever.

But the main thing was that we completed the store and it met our needs perfectly. We had a giant walk-in freezer—something we had lacked in Shirley's—with one door to the retail side and another opening into the ample storage area. Inspired by another one of our competitors in the Sunset District, Hoo's, we called our new store Moo's. And with the help of a commercial artist we created a cute sign: a cow's head, the two eyes of which were also the two "o"s in the name.

And then we got ready for the grand opening. As a promotion we offered a three-pound, half-gallon container containing fourteen percent butterfat for only ninety-nine cents. To advertise it, we hired kids from the nearby high school to distribute fliers door to door throughout Richmond. On the big day, a Saturday in the spring of 1952, the crowd was so large we could hardly make our way to the front of the line in order to open the door. And the demand for this cheap luxury never let up. Within a month the ten-gallon cans for cream we thought necessary proved inadequate and we installed a five hundred-gallon cork-insulated tank so large it looked like it belonged on an oil truck. Pipes connected this reservoir of cream to the machines, and then the finished product went right into one end of the freezer and was sold out the other. We had an efficient assembly line going, a factory of frozen treats.

It was highly lucrative, far outstripping the profits we made in San Francisco. But within a decade Paul and I would sell Moo's and leave the ice cream business. Sometimes I think we had barely gotten started at that point and could have built a national or international franchise out of it along the lines of Ben and Jerry's or Häagen-Dazs. We had an almost addictive product (made from my grandmother's recipe, I used to joke), an easy, effective method of producing it, the right way of packaging it, and not least of all a catchy name. In fact, after a while kids didn't ask their mothers for an ice cream anymore. Instead, the demand I heard was "Mommy, I want a Moo."

About a year after Moo's opened I noticed a corner lot for sale five blocks from the store and found out it was zoned for multiple residential units. Close to marrying Eda by this time, and wanting to live near my work, I bought it with the intention of putting up a fourplex and living in one flat and renting out the other three. Still in my twenties, and not yet a citizen, I was going to be a landlord.

The government-imposed limits on costs were now gone, but to build something from scratch was a major undertaking nonetheless. It would have been much easier just to purchase a small apartment house. But I had caught the development bug while erecting Moo's and learned a good deal about construction. From my experience in obtaining the loan to acquire Shirley's, I also knew a little about financing.

For my contractor I hired a likeable Norwegian named Carl, whose workmanship met the highest standards. After our maiden voyage together, I became his limited partner on various projects, investing some of my profits from Moo's in the construction of other residential properties and later public buildings.

Skilled though he was, Carl had no head for business. He allowed subcontractors to get away with inflated bids while he underestimated his own expenses and quoted clients unrealistically low prices. In building a private house, he would redo the entire paint job at no extra charge simply because the customer, who had chosen the color in the first place, didn't like the way it turned out.

But worst of all was Carl's slavish obedience to the architect's plans. One time the specifications called for tall, thin boards known as shiplap (since they overlapped one another) to hold the concrete for the foundation. Once the concrete dried, the wood was to be stripped and then used on the roof. Although I was a novice builder at that point, common sense told me the shiplap was too long and brittle to be peeled off in big enough pieces. Most of it would crack and have to be thrown away. Plywood, I strongly suggested, which was more flexible and came in manageable sizes, would be better for both the foundation and later for the roof. But Carl would not bring up the issue with the architect, whose blueprints he regarded like the Holy Bible. As I feared, we lost almost all the shiplap and had to buy a large amount of new plywood for the roof. Because of costly mistakes like these, the profit came to only three thousand dollars for an eighteen-month-long project, a new school for which the town of Pinole had paid millions.

I let Carl keep all of our paltry gain. I didn't have the heart to ask him for the portion due me. But I told him that our roles would have to change. I was no longer willing to be his partner, but I offered to be his employer. He agreed, and it was a much better arrangement for all concerned. I would select and purchase the site, negotiate with the subs, and, if need be, contend with the architect. Carl would concentrate on construction, where his talent lay, and be assured of a good-sized paycheck.

Now we began to develop properties differently. All over Richmond and nearby El Cerrito I'd buy lots, put up high quality eight- or twelve-unit apartment houses, rent them out, then sell them. They were all made to last, and I knew we had created something valuable when I saw other *builders* bidding on our finished product. It soon became even more profitable and exciting than Moo's.

Paul and I, meanwhile, were drifting apart. He married before I did, and his wife exerted a great influence on him, even in business, and increasingly I found myself at odds with both of them. He, too, went into real estate and did extremely well, but he specialized in trailer parks, something that held no attraction for me. Although we were still partners in Moo's, there was a growing sense of competition between us as we each pursued our separate deals.

Yet the changing relationship between Paul and me was only one reason why, with Eda's encouragement, I decided to sell Moo's about seven years after we were married and turn to development full-time. What counted most was my passion for building, and she and I could both see the promise it held. It would allow me to use my creativity more than I could in any retail business—to make something from nothing, shaping it the way I wanted. And I took much pride in the end result because I knew the high caliber of materials and craftsmanship that had gone into it. True, I was not well suited for every aspect of the occupation of developer. Even in later years I wasn't comfortable having to stand before a zoning commission or a redevelopment agency, with perhaps a hundred people in the audience, to argue the case for one of my projects. But my ability in detecting hidden value, my willingness to take risks, and my readiness to adapt to changing circumstances would serve me well.

Of course I had had no formal training in this field. But with my big brother Simcha, I had traded livestock in Poland. I had made my living after the war on the high wire of Europe's black market and had succeeded with two ice cream stores and some real estate in California. I felt I could trust my instincts. And, if it did not work out? Well, I didn't feel I had that much on the line since I never aspired to great wealth. I knew that whatever happened I would always be able to afford a meal at Kwan's for fifty cents.

Sadly, Paul and I would see little of each other during the decades that followed. But we had been so close during one of the most intense and pivotal periods in our lives—making the huge leap from being refugees in war-ravaged Munich to entrepreneurs in the booming Bay Area—that I would think about him all the time. We were together when we first made our way in America; he was by my side when I learned how to read the signs.

By the mid-1950s I was a family man. I readily adjusted to this phase of life, and it changed me profoundly. Eda, with her French and American schooling, love of the arts, and elegant sense of style, helped put me in touch with some of the finer things in life that I had missed during my hectic first years in America.

She also played a role in my business. Before we were married, Eda worked downtown as an executive secretary in the Bank of California. She always promised to bring me some "free samples" that I'm still waiting for. But what she did provide was good advice. From her vantage point in the real estate division, she could sometimes tell me which neighborhoods in the Bay Area were on the rise. I was tentative before making my first acquisition in Marin County, a parcel that I had eyed near the entrance to the exclusive Kent Woodlands section. Her emphatic approval tipped the scales in favor of my going ahead with the deal. Later, even with the responsibilities of being a mother and a part-time secretary for the Richmond School District, she would be deeply involved in the day-to-day management of some of my holdings: keeping the books, leasing the apartments, and showing the buildings when we put them up for sale. She was also a pretty good ice cream scooper at Moo's.

We were married on September 20, 1953, by a rabbi whom Eda knew, Saul White, one of the most dynamic spiritual leaders in the city. A learned East European immigrant, he had been ordained in New York and for almost two decades had built up a Conservative congregation, Beth Sholom, in San Francisco's Richmond District. But the ceremony, held on the day after Yom Kippur, was a low-key event. We took our vows in front of just a handful of people—Eda's sister and several close friends, not even including Paul Sade—in the rabbi's home. Afterwards we held a reception for a larger group in a modest hall on Geary Boulevard. That evening the two of us shared a meal at one of our favorite Chinese restaurants before spending our wedding night in the Claremont Hotel in the East Bay hills. For our honeymoon we took a few days off and drove down the coastal highway as far as Santa Barbara.

Our mood, particularly during the wedding ceremony, was almost unemotional. But this is what we had sought, thinking that the lack of feeling was preferable to the deep sorrow that would have engulfed us had Eda walked down the aisle in a fancy white dress. A big wedding would have highlighted the absence at the occasion of all but one of our family members.

Eda, born and raised in the ancient German town of Cologne on the Rhine, was part of an observant Jewish family even larger than mine. There were seven children, and neither her parents nor four of her siblings survived the war. Among four brothers, all older than she, only one was still alive. He had made aliyah and at the time of our wedding was the official driver for Foreign Minister (and soon to be Premier) Moshe Sharett. Later, as Joseph Tadmor, my brother-in-law would make a distinguished career as an Israeli diplomat. Eda's two other adult brothers escaped the Nazi net only to meet tragic deaths later on. One, a soldier in the Jewish Brigade, drowned when his ship, returning to Palestine from Italy, was torpedoed. The other, who fled to Holland and then reached England where he volunteered as a pilot in an auxiliary wing of the RAF, was shot down on a bombing run over Germany.

Eda and her older sister Henni had been smuggled over the French border in March 1939 and they were cared for in the exceptionally well run OSE (pronounced "Ozay") children's homes, first in the suburbs of Paris and later near Vichy, the capital of unoccupied France. But the rescuer who had brought them out of Cologne (a distant relative who had married France's Chief Rabbi) felt that the youngest brother and sister in the family— Solly was fourteen and Hanah was six in 1939—didn't quite fit the descriptions on the false papers she was carrying. She decided that it would be unsafe to take them across the frontier with Eda and Henni. So two children made it out but two were left behind.

They remained with their mother—Eda's father had been deported to Poland four months earlier just before *Kristallnacht*—and both parents, the boy, and the little girl were ultimately ghettoized and killed, likely in one of the death camps. Their precise fate could never be determined.

After two and a half years in France, Eda and Henni miraculously received visas to the United States. But they had a difficult adolescence on the West Coast, shuffled around from San Francisco's Homewood Terrace orphanage to a series of foster homes until they were old enough to be on their own. Like me, my wife had a youth filled with grief and the complicated, haunting feelings that have come to be known as survivor guilt.

The birth of our first child, Debra, in 1955, did a lot to help us regain a normal existence. The new life we brought forth—and we would have two more girls, Karen and Becky, and then a boy, David, over the next eleven years—could not replace the dozen immediate family members that together we lost. Nor could it restore the sense of the world being a safe place that we had felt in our large, nurturing families when we were small children ourselves. But becoming parents did much to put us back into the natural rhythm of things. Once we had a child, we felt we had taken a big step toward being like everyone else.

After Debbie was born we moved into a fine home that I built in the El Cerrito hills overlooking the bay. Fewer than ten years had passed since I had come through Ellis Island, and already I had an enormous amount to be thankful for. I had a life partner teaching me something new every day and a perfect little girl delighting us in ways we had not thought possible. In my early thirties, I owned a thriving business, held an array of good real estate investments, and was embarked upon a promising career as a developer. In the decades to come I would climb higher than any of the gypsy fortune-tellers in the Biala Podlaska marketplace could have foretold. Even in the 1950s it was clear to me that America and I were a match exceeding all expectations.

Yet with every successive triumph and every new joy, I felt a pain in my heart in not being able to share my life with any of the Epelbaums. I had been the underachiever, the problem child back in Poland. Now I so much wanted to show them that I had not turned out badly after all. They would have had to see it to believe it, but that was a satisfaction I could never know. The horrible fate of my family in Volhynia left me with emptiness the size of the universe. I got ahead during the day, but I remained in torment at night.

ELEVEN

A *Time To Build*

IF THERE IS ONE SYMBOL IN MY MIND of the unlimited promise of America, it is the Golden Gate Bridge. Built in defiance of the Depression, it is a work of beauty and strength that required ingenuity and daring. As a newly arrived immigrant back in 1947, all it took was a photo of that landmark—on a poster I saw in a bus terminal on a blustery day in Chicago—to propel me across the plains and over the mountains to the Pacific Coast.

Now, I need only look out my own windows to be inspired by that man-made wonder because in the early 1990s Eda and I moved into a co-op in San Francisco with a view of the Presidio, the Marina, the Marin Headlands, and, of course, the Golden Gate. Gazing from my living room at the bridge that many said could never be built I've often contemplated my long upward climb as a developer in the Bay Area, a career as unlikely as my survival in Nazi-occupied Europe.

People familiar with how little I started with often ask me how I did it. Well, I don't know of any magic formula. As with any high-stakes business, I had to persevere when misfortune struck. But I had to be an innovator, too. Although I learned a lot from others, I also had to be ready to do things differently when the situation called for it.

This was certainly the case during my first decade as a full-time developer, the 1960s, when I focused on Marin County where I would construct almost a thousand high-quality housing units in half a dozen towns. I have been incredibly lucky, of course. My deep involvement in Marin has coincided with a spectacular boom making it one of the choicest areas in California. But the wealthy little county also poses serious problems for builders compared with other parts of the Bay Area. The winter rains are heavy and mudslides are a constant danger. The absence of the Bay Area Rapid Transit system has added to the ordeal of commuting and certainly made the area less pleasant. And while I have been committed to the preservation of open spaces, I've nevertheless been stymied at times by strong anti-growth forces here: government agencies, publicity-seeking politicians, and even private foundations. I learned that bureaucrats will block a major housing project due to an endangered species on the land—a butterfly or a mouse—and even because of a particular kind of grass.

The large number of different municipalities I've had to deal with has also been problematic. There are about a dozen villages, towns, and small cities, each with its own council and commissions, in a county of fewer than a quarter million people. I have been able to get around the various obstacles that have arisen in each jurisdiction, but it has taken every ounce of my patience and determination.

The ups and downs of doing business in Marin were evident in my first project, the property on Kent Avenue near Kent Woodlands that I bought with Eda's encouragement. Aware that my land was in a flood zone, I hired a soils engineer to conduct a series of tests. He shocked me with his recommendation. Because I owned a virtual swamp, he said, the only way to develop it would be to drive long piles deep into the ground for the units to sit on. Even with my limited experience I knew that pile driving could shake the nearby houses off their foundations. I would face a barrage of lawsuits even before I built one apartment. Anxiously, I sought a second opinion from another expert. Indeed, there was a layer of muck on the property three feet thick, he said. But it could be hauled away (provided it didn't leak out the beds of the dump trucks) and be replaced with fill that would support the foundations for structures of at least two stories. Not an ideal situation, I thought, but a big improvement over what I had feared.

Now it was time to hire an architect. Always eager to check out the competition, I visited a nearby apartment complex in Kentfield, at the time the only one in Marin with a swimming pool, and I liked the look of the buildings and the way they were arranged on the wooded site. I found out that it was the design of the young Dick Olmstead, of the firm of Hooper, Olmstead and Emmons, and I immediately put him to work on my project, which would also have the status symbol of the pool. But I added an important proviso: much larger rooms. In renting out my apartment houses in the East Bay I had learned that people were often turned off by tiny bedrooms and kitchens. With lumber and other construction materials reasonably priced in those days, it really didn't cost that much more to build larger units. Besides, you obtained a permit from the city for a set number of apartments, regardless of the square footage of each one. So there was no reason to scrimp on the size. But one of Olmstead's senior colleagues disagreed with me. He believed in building houses with bedrooms just large enough to meet FHA standards, something

*At work with Roger Hooper (of the architectural
firm of Hooper, Olmstead and Emmons)*

like eight feet by nine feet. In fact, this is even how he designed
his own expensive home in Kent Woodlands. For him, a bedroom
was a place where you turn off the lights and go to sleep. I stuck
to my opinion, though, and felt vindicated years later when the
prominent architect went to sell his house and had to enlarge the
bedrooms to attract buyers.

But Olmstead understood me and began working on the plans
for a thirty-unit complex, two and half times as large as anything
I had built before. With the winter floods in mind—people actually floated down Kent Avenue by boat in those years—he placed
the garages on the lower level so that when the creek overflowed
it would cause a minimum of damage. Although it was a good
scheme, I feared I had taken on too big and complicated a project.

I had many sleepless nights before breaking ground. No longer by my side was Carl, my reliable contractor in the East Bay. In the shift to Marin I decided to be my own contractor, which I could do as the owner of the property even though I did not yet have a license. I did employ a capable and trusted foreman, Bob Tatum, to whom I gave a lot of latitude, but now I doubted the wisdom of the whole enterprise.

Olmstead designed three appealing buildings for me, each on a different elevation, but there was no way to avoid placing four apartments on the level of the creek. Sure enough, they were flooded the first winter but I was relieved to see that the tenants loved the place so much they didn't move out. With our help, they would just clean up after each big storm.

About a year after construction, and with the project fully leased, I put it on the market. A local doctor and his broker came over, stood in the courtyard near the pool, and didn't even ask to inspect any of the units. They simply wrote up an offer for my list price.

It was proof to me that there was something special about southern Marin. Physically, western Contra Costa County, where I had gotten my start in real estate while my day job was ice cream making, wasn't that different. El Cerrito also had bay views, lovely trees, and a mild climate. But the proximity to the Pacific Ocean and the Redwood Highway, the Golden Gate Bridge and the city of San Francisco set Marin apart. So it wasn't long before I built a much larger complex—eighty units—a half mile south of the Kent Avenue property in Larkspur. I had also learned something by then about economy of scale: a bigger project, because it warrants an on-site manager, can be easier to deal with than a smaller one.

I named it Woodlark, a complex that won acclaim, even from other architects, for its imaginative design. Olmstead had come through for me again. Proceeding meticulously to fit the buildings to the land, his final product was seamless. He ingeniously preserved the redwoods and made sure that most of the units would have bay views; he allowed an abundance of sunlight to enter and created a spacious indoor-outdoor feeling. I could see that *his style*, blending modern, classical, and rustic features, would not go *out of style.*

I was so impressed that I soon commissioned Olmstead to design my own home in nearby San Rafael for our growing family. Eda and I still live in it today, dividing our time between the city and the suburbs. Forty years on, it's lost none of its charm.

As big as it seemed to me at the time, Woodlark was merely the prelude for a much larger project. On adjacent land to the south, a forty-five acre hillside also overlooking the bay, I developed Skylark, a complex eventually numbering five hundred and fifty apartments and townhouses.

It began modestly. I first bought a plot of only five acres along Magnolia Avenue with no firm idea of what I would do with it. I simply figured that in the future I would tie that piece, which sat in the shadow of a tall ridge, to something else. Soon I was pleasantly surprised to find that the entire hillside behind my site was zoned for multiple residential development. A local contractor owned a twenty-five-acre parcel on it, but not being an experienced developer he was reluctant to build on the giant, steep slope.

He agreed to sell me his land, and now I owned thirty acres in all, from the avenue to the hilltop. I was getting somewhere. But it soon became clear from the surveyors' reports that if I wanted to put together the large, contiguous tract needed for a major development, I was still missing one "piece of the pie"—a fifteen-acre, wedge-shaped plot with its wide side on level ground and its tip all the way up on the hill. This lot was essential, not only to knit my holdings together but also to satisfy the authorities' requirement of a roadway into the development at least sixty feet wide. Escalle Drive, right off Magnolia Avenue, already appeared on the map on the very edge of my property, but it was only thirty feet across. To broaden it, I needed that much width again. It had to be either in my hands or the city's for me to proceed, and it sat within the fifteen-acre lot I lacked.

Who owned that last vital piece? It was Adolph Tiscornia, one the most colorful characters I have ever encountered. A crusty Italian in his mid-seventies, he was a large man who had been a boxer in his youth and had a lot of fight left in him. I was awed by how much land he controlled. During the Depression his close friend, the legendary A. P. Giannini, founder of Bank of America, had advanced him the funds to buy at auction hundreds of acres all over Larkspur, prime property that was now worth a fortune. But Tiscornia lived so frugally that he sometimes wore clothes made out of potato sacks. His office, on a valuable site he owned in downtown Larkspur, was housed in a grimy old building that was part of a defunct winery.

A lonely widower whose only child had been killed in an airplane crash, Tiscornia, partly deaf, was a nonstop talker. Often he would ramble on for a half hour about some adventure in his past, barely pausing to draw a breath. During one phone conversation I was so annoyed by his endless patter that I put the receiver on my desk, ate my lunch, and picked up the phone to find him still chattering away. Sometimes he had a running dialogue with his car radio, with the volume turned up, not only talking to the news announcer but also yelling at him.

The feisty Tiscornia had his own fantasies about developing the land between my two tracts so, rather than ask him to sell it to me, I tried persuading him to donate the small strip along Escalle Drive (a little more than an eighth of an acre) to the city. A widened road would be better for both of us builders, I told him, and furthermore, I pointed out, he would be entitled to a reduction in his property taxes. I argued my case over a long series of lunches in a restaurant he liked in San Francisco. He owned the adjoining parking lot and had installed his own meters. Before we'd go in to eat, he would empty a few of the boxes and then pay the bill with the pocketful of quarters he'd taken out. But even though we met countless times, it was tough to convince him of my plan. Month after month passed and while he showed some interest, it seemed that all he wanted to do was talk.

Then one morning he called me at home with his usual brusque greeting of "Hey, Pell." I braced myself for a long monologue, but for once he kept it short. He was ready to deed the land along Escalle Drive to the city. In bed with a sore throat, I got up anyway and drove over to meet him at the courthouse to assist in the transfer. If I was sick, Tiscornia seemed near death. He could barely walk, and all the color had drained from his face. He told me that while taking coins out of his parking meters in San Francisco someone walked up behind him, hit him in the head, and knocked him down. Tiscornia fought back, flattened the guy, and then called the police, who took the unlucky mugger away. But the gruff old prizefighter would never be the same and passed away within the month. I realized then that he must have known that he didn't have long to live and wanted to do a big favor for me while he still could.

But while the right-of-way was no longer a problem, I still needed the rest of the fifteen acres. Tiscornia had willed almost all of his vast estate to his longtime secretary, who was eager to dispose of the properties. To my surprise she turned out to be a tough negotiator, first offering to sell me the land for two hundred thousand dollars and then, at the last minute, raising the price to a quarter million, almost twice per acre what I had paid about a year earlier. My attorney and I were stunned to learn that Tiscornia had bought the parcel for a mere fifteen hundred dollars in 1940. But I had no alternative. I had to pay the lady what she demanded.

At last I was ready to start building. My architect was Dick Olmstead, of course, and the huge, rugged hill of Skylark, only two miles east of Marin's most beloved natural landmark, Mt. Tamalpais, presented him with the broadest canvas yet for his talents. He soon conceived a layered, or terraced, contour for the site, affording almost all the units sweeping bay or mountain views. He had deep reverence for the many redwood, oak, and bay trees, and actually outdid his masterly design of Woodlark.

With enthusiasm I began the first phase, about a hundred units on the flat part of the site between Magnolia Avenue and the base of the hill. But as soon as we broke ground I became quite distressed by what we uncovered. Only two or three feet below the grass and shrubs were enormous boulders of the hardest rock imaginable. I found out that they had been rolled down from the top of the hill many years earlier by the former owner to plug up the giant holes made when he had excavated the land to provide fill for another project.

We needed to remove the boulders, which proved to be one of the most frustrating problems in my entire career as a developer. I finally found a working quarry in Marin willing to take the "blue rock" as it is commonly called. "Have I got something for you!" I informed the owner. Although he agreed to pay for the trucks to haul it off my property, I was responsible for loading it. Yet the boulders, some the size of small houses, were too big and heavy to be lifted onto trucks and carted away. The massive blue rock had to be broken up first, and for that we brought a crane with a wrecking ball onto the site. The stone was so hard that it damaged the machinery. Some of the metal parts became embedded in the boulders, making our task even more difficult and hazardous. It was all I could do to keep the rock-crushing company on the job; several times the boss wanted to quit.

Meanwhile, we were digging into the hill to carve out the "shelves" needed for the units of the next phase. Our concept was to use the displaced earth from the heights to fill in the gaping holes left by the boulders on the lower level. But a winter storm suddenly turned this mountain of dirt into a river of mud. It flowed, or oozed, all the way down to Magnolia Avenue and Escalle, now known as Skylark Drive, blocking traffic in all directions. Luckily, this was a period when city officials, in need of permit fees, were still generally sympathetic to builders—God only knows the trouble I'd be in if something like that happened today—and they came out to help me deal with it. In fact, the city manager himself, in high rubber boots, shoveled mud off the road. And this wasn't the only disaster. During the grading of the site, we were plagued by mudslides, sometimes so powerful they uprooted mature trees and carried them down the hill. When the big downpours came, I would drive over in the middle of the night, if necessary, to supervise the cleanup. Rain meant pain.

There were other rough moments, but I never let go of my vision of creating something unique in that special place. After the first phase was completed we built three hundred and fifty-four units on the hillside. Like those below they were designed with decks, fireplaces, high gabled ceilings, clerestory windows and, of course, my trademark feature, unusually large rooms. A two-bedroom apartment measured eleven hundred and forty square feet. We also equipped each unit with top-of-the-line appliances, and once Skylark was finished I took great care to find the most capable people to manage and maintain it. I intended to offer my neighbors not merely functional boxes to live in, but rather something of lasting quality, homes in harmony with the natural setting just north of the Golden Gate Bridge.

During the years I was constructing residential complexes in Marin I would often have lunch on Saturday afternoons with my foreman, Bob Tatum, at an eatery in San Rafael. Once we overheard two guys at the next table discussing the local real estate picture. One of them, a broker, told the other about a developer who was having great success erecting handsome apartment buildings in prime locations. He went on and on, and it soon became clear that the subject of their conversation was me. Hoping he would switch to another topic, I said nothing and just continued my conversation with Bob.

We all got up to leave at the same time, though, and on the way out I introduced myself to the broker. "I'm the guy you've been talking about for the last half-hour," I said. He was flustered at first but seemed glad to meet me, and we soon took a liking to each other. Roger Bohne (his family name had been Cohen) was the son of one of the first Jews to play in the major leagues; San Francisco-born Sammy Bohne had been a scrappy infielder for the St. Louis Cardinals as early as 1916. Roger, well-connected in the Bay Area business world, stayed in close touch and a few years later called me with a fascinating proposition.

It was late 1973, with the country deep in recession and Washington paralyzed by the Watergate scandal. Roger was representing two of Northern California's biggest developers, Bill Wilson and Miller Ream, who were now in a predicament, and he saw an opportunity for them and for me. They had recently completed a large park of fine office buildings on the Peninsula, but in the economic downturn were having a tough time leasing it up and meeting their mortgage payments. They needed to unload some of their properties and raise cash fast.

When Bohne offered to show me one of their office buildings, I was ambivalent because nearly all of my experience had been on the residential side of the real estate business. Except for my own ice cream store years earlier, I had never built or even owned commercial units. But my doubts disappeared the minute I walked into the property they had for sale. It was an almost new, seventy-five-thousand-square-foot structure, with an ample parking lot, on a hill in San Mateo overlooking the bay.

You could almost say I fell in love with it. I was intoxicated by that newly built smell that some people can't resist in an automobile fresh from the factory, by the hum of activity in the offices (though only a portion of them were occupied), and above all by the mighty mass of concrete that made the edifice seem taller and more imposing than its three stories. Compared to this, I told myself, I've been building with wooden sticks. I knew, too, that renting out such a property would be a new experience. My tenants would not be families that might complain about the plumbing or the paint job. They would be big companies that would sign leases for five or ten years; it would be a deal between one businessman and another. All in all, I felt that this represented a higher plateau. It would be like the jump I had made more than a decade earlier, from selling ice cream to constructing apartment houses.

But how to acquire that first office building for which they wanted several million? Like almost everyone else in the mid-seventies, I was not sitting on a lot of cash. And I have always been careful not to overburden myself with debt, a major mistake I had seen many developers make. Too many builders overextended themselves in the good years—when the banks were more than happy to oblige them—and then were wiped out when the inevitable lean times arrived. I have done the opposite, often surprising a loan officer by taking only a portion of what his financial institution was willing to lend. In this case, I could assume the debt on the property that Wilson and Ream were carrying, and for the balance trade my equity in another project.

What I could appreciate only later was that I had opened the door to much more than a single office building. My contact with Bill Wilson and especially Miller Ream increased over the next decade, and one or both of them brought me into many of their largest deals—numerous properties in downtown San Francisco and elsewhere.

Through them I was able to take a major position in the city's South of Market Street district, still a gritty, industrial section in the 1970s that was destined to be a lively center for business and the arts. Despite the residential complexes I had built, I knew little about putting up lofty office buildings. But my new partners had their own construction company, Webcor, which had a superb track record, so I figured it was a safe bet to go in with them. It was very different than building in Marin when I personally had to supervise operations, often on a muddy hillside, almost every day. Wilson and Ream were also adept at leasing commercial property and managing it. I sat back and got a detailed statement every month and a nice check quarterly.

And yet I was hardly a passive investor. In addition to my capital, I contributed needed advice and encouragement. Wilson in particular was a major player. The subject of numerous articles in the local press, he would later build the headquarters for Oracle in Redwood Shores and come very close to buying Rockefeller Center. But unlike me, he and Ream had gotten hurt in the downward economic slide of the mid-seventies and were frequently gun shy when a big new deal presented itself. They would collect a handsome management fee during the life of a partnership, but typically they would retain an ownership position of only ten percent or even less for themselves, syndicating a project among many outside investors to lessen their own risk. I was more aggressive, not only taking a bigger piece for myself but also pushing the entire venture forward. To me, downtown San Francisco property seemed like a no-lose proposition as the city's old manufacturing sector gave way to more and more white-collar jobs in finance, insurance, real estate, and trade with other Pacific Rim countries. The value of prime office space, I assured them, was bound to rise in the years ahead.

Ultimately, Bill Wilson and Miller Ream each went his own way. I remained closer to Miller, the more easygoing of the two and a man generous toward everyone around him. He would later face a series of debilitating personal problems, but for about a decade we spent a lot of time together, developing property in the Bay Area and traveling around the country to find other promising locations. He had grown up on a farm in Iowa, and I even partnered with him in constructing an office building in Des Moines. I thought it was his way of saying to the local folks that he had made good, but it was one of the few things we did jointly that didn't pan out.

We also sold one of our prime San Francisco buildings too soon, in 1989, an office tower for which I thought we had gotten a great price, but one that almost doubled in value a decade later. It still bothers me. Yet it is not for the usual reasons that I felt sorry about missing out on the big gain that came in the nineties. I already had more money than my family would ever need, and my goal had never been a Donald Trump-type lifestyle. Not only don't I have my own jet, I feel self-indulgent just flying first class. But I do admit that I got caught up in the "game" of wheeling and dealing and nurtured a keen competitiveness that went far beyond mere money and material possessions. Perhaps I was spurred on by the friendly rivalry Paul Sade and I developed while still partners at Moo's. Or maybe it goes back further to the intensity my brother Simcha and I felt when we were trading cattle in Polish villages before the war. When it came to business, we played to win.

So I do look back with regret at the great deals that got away. As well as I've done, there have also been enough examples of bad timing and missed opportunities to fill a whole book by themselves. Eda doesn't understand how I can continue to kick myself over some of these mistakes. I suppose she's right, but I don't think I will ever get over one error in particular—my failure to enter the New York real estate market in the mid-1970s.

The fabulous metropolis that had enthralled me as a young immigrant in 1947 hit bottom a quarter century later, mired in crime and unemployment, municipal debt and a declining tax base. Many businesses were leaving town for the suburbs or the Sun Belt, and skyscrapers in Lower Manhattan, some of them with their doors boarded up, were on the block for bargain-basement prices. But you didn't have to be a genius to predict that a city with the resources and vitality of New York would eventually rebound. And, indeed, office towers in good locations that were offered at thirty dollars a square foot would fetch ten times that price a dozen years later. Not since the Dutch bought the island from the Indians was there a better time to invest.

Miller and I had the chance to acquire an enormous property that was virtually being given away. Set on a knoll just north of New York City and overlooking the Hudson, it consisted of about a million and a half square feet of office space on a parcel of more than three hundred acres. It was in foreclosure, and the bank that had taken it back was eager to find a buyer to assume its twenty-four-million-dollar loan. Miller and I flew to Chicago, where the bank was headquartered, and its president was waiting for us on the sidewalk as our limousine pulled up at eight o'clock in the evening. He ushered us into his office and, after a lot of pleasantries, explained we could simply take over the project with nothing down.

Now it was time to go on to New York and inspect the property. The buildings, though largely leased, were in need of some repair, but I focused more on the possibilities of developing all that vacant land. Feeling bullish, I signaled my willingness to go ahead with the deal, and we were whisked off to a meeting in a plush boardroom in Rockefeller Center to negotiate the details of the purchase.

The New York brokers proposed to manage and lease the property for five percent ownership on top of the customary fees, a costly but convenient arrangement, I thought, since Miller and I were based three thousand miles away. But Miller wanted the brokers to have some "skin in the game." He insisted that if they were to receive an equity position they should put in a good chunk of their sales commission as a further indication of their commitment. This they refused to do and he angrily walked out. Even though we remained in New York several more days—while Miller got back into good humor by enjoying the city's exciting nightlife, and I sat around in frustration—the deal fell apart and we went home empty-handed.

These were the very years that the Reichmann family, Orthodox Jews from Toronto, bought up depressed Manhattan buildings, laying the foundation for a multi-billion-dollar international empire. It was also the shot I had to become one of the biggest developers in America. Yet despite the monkey wrench that Miller threw into the deal, it would be foolish for me to blame him. I could have purchased that office park on the Hudson on my own and gained a solid foothold in the Big Apple. But this was such a major undertaking that even I lacked the guts, to say nothing of the experience that was needed.

And so I was not to become a New York real estate mogul, which at least spared me the unwanted media attention that would have come with it. I passed up other mammoth acquisitions, too, such as half of the real estate portfolio of the Chrysler Corporation when it was facing bankruptcy in the early 1980s, including valuable land in the Bay Area near both the San Francisco and San Jose airports.

Although I shied away from the megadeals, I did add substantially to my holdings in Northern California in the eighties and early nineties. Now on my own for the first time in the San Francisco office building arena, I erected an attractive six-story structure south of Market with a travertine skin, gleaming metal bands around it, a gorgeous Italian marble entrance way, and decks on the top floor. My daughter Debbie, who worked for me in those years, had a lot to do with the building's allure. Not only does she have an eye for design, but like me she also felt that using the highest-grade materials was the best business decision we could make.

But it was located on Harrison Street—much further south and in a rougher patch of SoMa than many developers thought prudent for a top-of-the-line edifice. Strangely enough, we even had to fight the city on this point. They had already approved the badly conceived plans of a man who had an option on the site, drawings that called for a hulking, stucco enclosure, one entire side of which was to be flush with the property line and without windows! The young city planners preferred that monstrosity to our open, airy design because they thought that inferior buildings would serve to keep rents low. All we want to attract there are "back office" operations, they told us, and I wondered why a book-keeper, say, was less entitled to a window and a pleasant working environment than anyone else. We had to come back to the planning department countless times before they finally approved our concept.

By the time we finished construction in 1990, the rental market had softened markedly. Still, I could see that the property, which faced the key thoroughfare of Second Street, where we placed an entrance as well, would be squarely in the path of the downtown expansion once the economy recovered. The newly built Moscone Convention Center and then the Yerba Buena Center for the Arts added luster to the neighborhood, and residential high-rises that went up in nearby South Beach brought many more retail businesses into the area, improving it further. We leased our building, and I feel that I have been a pioneer in a district that lately has become one of the most dynamic in the city. I followed my instincts and not the crowd's. Often the time to build, I knew, is when everyone else is on the sidelines.

In the late eighties I also began to focus on a different type of property. Livermore, an almost rural town in the eastern reaches of Alameda County, was about as far from big-city excitement as one could get. But around the time it became a bedroom community of the sprawling Bay Area I started to develop a large stretch of land there—my first foray into retail and industrial buildings.

It would be one of my most profitable projects, but I almost missed out on buying the site. It all began when a broker called me regarding a hundred-acre parcel near an exit of the 580 freeway, about twenty miles east of Hayward. I drove out to see it.

Although I arrived after dark, I could tell it was well located. To start with, it faced the busy main artery into the center of Livermore. Not far away was the booming town of Pleasanton. And new streets alongside the tract itself were already being paved. But any interest I had in the property vanished when the broker told me the price—sixteen million dollars—way too high, I thought, for something in the boondocks.

But a month later he called again. He reached me just before I was about to leave my office for the day and said that the land, now in foreclosure, would be auctioned off the next morning on the steps of the Oakland courthouse. Smelling a bargain, I called up my banker, Grant Heller at Bank of America, and told him that I needed three hundred thousand dollars in cashier's checks, in fifty-thousand-dollar increments. To bid at such an auction one had to have ten percent of the down payment in hand, and somehow I had the feeling that I could win the property for three million, a discount of more than eighty percent.

Grant moved quickly to get the checks and met my broker and me when the auction began at 10 A.M. Only two other bidders were there but before long the price was up to two and a half million. Then one of them, a well-dressed, middle-aged man, came over to me and whispered that for a hundred thousand dollars he would walk away. I half-admired his chutzpah and for a moment thought of how, as a kid, I had seen Simcha shake down rival buyers of livestock in this way. I felt I knew this fellow's game. Of course I refused to pay him off. It would have corrupted the entire process, and I didn't even see how it would help me that much since I still would not be the only bidder left.

He promptly dropped out, but the other guy soon went up to near the three-million-dollar mark. I could sense, though, that he was beginning to flag at that level and that I could probably get it for under three and a half. The problem was that I didn't have enough money on me for the down payment at that price. I could send Heller to a branch office of Bank of America in the East Bay for more cashier's checks, but he wouldn't be as well known as in San Francisco and it might take a while for him to return. The bidding was about to exceed three million at any moment!

Then I hit on the right delaying tactic. I remembered that at these auctions the legal description of the property, sometimes referred to as "metes and bounds," is usually read aloud at the beginning, and that hadn't been done in this case. I knew that this parcel consisted of dozens and dozens of smaller lots, some of them only a quarter of an acre in size. It might take hours for the whole recitation.

I went up to the auctioneer and told him it wasn't fair for us to be bidding on something that had not been precisely defined, and therefore I demanded to hear all the official language. He agreed but, not wanting to wear himself out, handed the thick sheaf of papers to my broker, who began to hold forth with all of the relish you would have reading a phone book. Now I turned to Grant Heller. Having bought some time, I told him to get three more checks for twenty-five thousand each. It took him over an hour, and he returned out of breath. But he needn't have rushed; the broker wasn't even halfway finished reading the legal descriptions. Though I felt sorry for the poor guy, because his outdoor oration was making him hoarse, I had to let him finish. Finally, the auction resumed. I won the property for three point four million.

If I had ever bought something on impulse, this was it. I hadn't even seen the place in daylight. But I sensed that I couldn't go too far wrong at this price. It's the kind of acquisition you can make when you're on your own like I am; when you're not accountable to a board of directors, shareholders, or even limited partners; when no one asks you to justify your purchase with a marketing survey or anything else.

Of course, when it came to developing the property I wondered what I had gotten myself into. I felt a little pathetic just putting up a sign on a hundred-acre vacant lot that said: "Will build to suit." But I did more than that. I met with the former owners and got their brochures and tenant leads and was soon encouraged to learn that the roads made possible by a recently passed bond issue were nearing completion.

And then my first tenant came along—Safeway. Almost all the property was zoned for industrial use, so the shopping center we now proposed to build required a variance from the planning commission. At the open meeting I was pleased by the strong turnout from the many housing complexes nearby, people who were tired of having to drive miles to the downtown Livermore stores every time they needed something. The residents stood up and complained that their public officials had neglected the area, and the rezoning was approved before my broker or attorney even needed to speak.

But things did not go that smoothly with Safeway, one of the very largest supermarket chains in North America. They seemed tentative about the project, and it took many months for my lawyers and their lawyers to work out the lease calling for us to construct a store for them on the site. Even after the agreement was signed, I heard rumors that they weren't sure about actually going forward. So I called up the person in charge and asked him to meet me for lunch near the property. I was accompanied by two of my kids: David, who was a college student at Berkeley at the time, and Debbie, who had graduated from Boston College Law School and was now in my employ.

The corporate executive towered over me; he must have been

six foot seven. And I think that reflected the kind of superiority he felt. While we were eating he expressed doubts that the area was ready for a Safeway. It seemed like he wanted a way out of the deal. Then, when we left the restaurant and stood around outside, he was blunt. We're not going to open here, he said, even if you build the store and even if we have to pay rent. "We'll just leave it vacant," he concluded. This was his way of trying to pressure me into letting the company out of its lease; he evidently figured that my bank might not grant the construction loan if it heard the anchor tenant was going to refuse to open its doors.

He didn't know that I was less in need of institutional financing than most developers. Aside from that, I was not about to cave in to such threats. I had to look up to talk to him, but I wouldn't allow myself to be cowed. Very conscious that my kids were hearing this interchange I told the guy in no uncertain terms that we were going to build the store. "You can do whatever you want with it," I said, "but we have a lease and you owe the rent. If you want to keep it empty, fine." David has reminded me of that conversation many times since, and I am glad it made a strong impression on my son. In the end Safeway did occupy the facility and I heard that among their roughly seventeen hundred outlets it turned out to be the second most profitable.

I think I'm a little quicker than most to see through the kind of smokescreen Safeway was laying down. Perhaps it goes back to my cattle trading days in the villages near Biala Podlaska when as a child I learned first hand the meaning of the term I would later hear in the States: "Let the buyer beware." And in Manievich, after our own neighbors betrayed us, it became impossible for me to be the trusting type. I grew to be skeptical of people and that became part of my approach to business. I would say the wariness has contributed to my success, but some, including my own kids, have told me that I've gone too far in that direction, that I am much too suspicious of others. Yet even if I wanted to, it is not something I can change.

TWELVE

My Family and My World

OF COURSE, I CANNOT EXPECT my four children, all raised in a sheltered suburb in Marin, to have the same attitudes toward life as I do. They've never experienced the hardships that many other Americans have had to face, let alone the hard day-to-day existence and later the stark terror that I knew in Poland and the Ukraine. They're generally optimistic and tend to see the best in people.

And this is what Eda and I hoped when we raised them, that they would not be naïve but also that they would not regard the world as a hostile place. We wanted each of them to have a normal childhood, if there is such a thing. So we didn't make our life stories the main topic of conversation every night when they were growing up. We didn't want to frighten or burden them with the pain we carried inside us.

This is not to say that we hid from them the terrible events in our past. Even as little kids they knew why we spoke with an accent, why none of their grandparents was alive, and why, even though we both came from large families, they had only one aunt and one uncle. Debbie, perhaps because she was raised closest in time to the catastrophe, is the one who has been most affected by it. When she was twelve her mother took her to New York to meet Dr. Ernst Papanek, the brilliant and compassionate educator who headed the network of children's homes that sheltered Eda during the war.

But the main point is that at least *consciously*—and I use that term because children can often sense things without being told directly—we did not make a major issue out of the Holocaust. And when we did speak of it, there was naturally a big difference between the stories of survivors like Eda and me and those who remained obsessed with the trauma for the rest of their lives because they had gone through the death camps. By contrast, I had spent almost a year and a half fighting back with a gun and in that sense my experience had some similarity with the men in the U.S. armed forces during the war—something that instilled pride in my kids rather than dread, shame, or pity. I think they saw me in a heroic light. I had been a victim, surely, but I was much more than that, too.

As for Eda, she had had to flee her home as a ten-year-old under terrifying circumstances, but she found a safe haven in France and received an excellent education there. Her losses, like mine, were incalculable, but she did not suffer bodily harm during those years. Her personal story was more remarkable for how she escaped than for what she endured. So both of our backgrounds contained some positive elements. Beyond that, as a young couple in America, we were more self-sufficient than most refugees and did not live in a community of survivors. It all served to buffer our children from the horrors of the Holocaust.

Yet there is no getting around the fact that we both had been traumatized by the murder of our loved ones and by being uprooted from our childhood homes. It had to have some effect on us as parents and influence our offspring. In Eda's case it made her more protective than most mothers. While we freely allowed our children to enjoy all manner of sports, she was overly careful when it came to supervising them on a playground or in a park. We were both more reluctant than other parents to leave the kids with others when they were small. Even now that they are adults, Eda makes a point of being in constant contact with them by phone. Some of this is simply because of the very close relationship we both have with them. But I also believe that she feels more anxiety about their safety than is necessary.

More interesting, though, is the way *our kids* have been overprotective of *us*. Adolescent rebellion, often fierce in the California suburbs, took a fairly mild form in our house. Obviously this is a complicated matter open to many explanations but it may be that, aware of the mental torment Eda and I had suffered, our youngsters held back from the kind of direct confrontation that has afflicted so many families.

But overall, I believe the impact of the Holocaust on the second generation has been exaggerated. In recent decades we have seen all sorts of memoirs and psychological studies, classes and encounter groups, claiming that being the child of a survivor is the key to an individual's personality and even the cause of someone's failure in life. That's something I cannot accept given that so many children face far worse problems, such as parents who are abusive or absent, and still lead productive lives. Maybe it's my no-nonsense nature, but I feel there is a whole industry of excuse-making that has grown up in America, and the "child of a survivor" complaint is a prime example.

Regarding my own kids, I believe their lives have been affected less by the Holocaust than by my financial success. Not in the sense that Eda and I spoiled them when they were small, giving in to their every desire. We did not live lavishly when they were growing up, and the large and comfortable home in which they were raised is neither a mansion nor in an exclusive neighborhood. The kids all attended public schools, and their friends, from every background, streamed in and out of our house all the time. But we departed from most other well-off parents by being very generous with our children when they entered adulthood, giving them a share of the business and thus providing them with an independent source of income. This may have reduced the pressure they might otherwise have felt to climb to the top of the career ladder. But it has also enabled them to pursue broader interests and to fulfill themselves in ways that might not have been possible until much later in their lives.

They all have professional degrees. Debra is an attorney; Karen has an MBA; Becky is an architect; and David has a Master's in education. But while they have worked in their respective fields, they've accomplished a lot in other areas as well. Debbie practiced law and was later employed by me but also used her uncommon motivational abilities as a lay leader of the local Jewish Community Federation. This led to a deep commitment to Israel. She has lived there for the past few years, raising her daughter Beronika, the Sabra in our family, and, with two Israeli partners, directing a company that invests in and manages start-ups. Karen, two years younger than Debbie, played every kind of sport as a kid. Now she follows the Giants and 49ers closely and, like me, is an avid golfer. She graduated from UC Berkeley, and then got her Master's in Business Administration from San Francisco State. After working for a real estate broker for a few years, she joined me at Pell Development and, more than the other kids, likes the day-to-day responsibilities and challenges of managing property. Now that I'm semiretired she is the boss of the company and can run it without me. Becky, our youngest daughter, was trained as an architect at Berkeley, and was hired by a New York firm where she showed much promise. But then she decided to be a full-time mom. She had met her future husband, Loren Kaplan, when they were ten-year-olds in the Sunday school of our temple in San Rafael. He became an orthodontist and they live not far from us with their three children: Alexander (our first grandkid who was born in 1992), Lindsay, and little Jeremy. Becky is president of the Osher Marin Jewish Community Center and has used her design skills to enhance the extensive facility's playgrounds.

Our youngest child, David, played varsity football in high school and delivered an inspirational speech at his commencement that people still talk about. He was the third Pell to graduate from Berkeley, where he fell in love with African American literature and developed a lifelong interest in race relations. Given his adventurous ways, I wasn't surprised when he went to New York (Greenwich Village, to be exact) to try to make it as a writer, a calling that he follows today, back in San Francisco, with a daily column on his website interpreting the world news for many thousands of people. A giving young man, he taught high school English for two years in a tough Brooklyn neighborhood and developed innovative extracurricular programs for disadvantaged youth. But he has also been a sports reporter for a local TV channel and in recent years an advisor/investor for dozens of new firms.

So our kids have done a lot of interesting things. But Eda and I have been most concerned, and most pleased, with their character development. I can't say that we followed any particular philosophy of parenting but we cared deeply about their problems, made very clear the difference between right and wrong, and tried to spend as much time with them as we could. The truth is that my busy schedule kept me from the family more than I wanted. Frequently I'd have to go out to a building site on Saturdays and

Clockwise from upper left: My children Becky, David, Karen, and Debra

Sundays, and, while at home, too often my mind was preoccupied with business matters. But I tried to make time for the kids, going to their sporting events and school performances, and taking them on vacations. When they were young we often went on family jaunts to places like Hawaii, Lake Tahoe, Disneyland, and Las Vegas. Until they were grown, Eda and I didn't leave them when we traveled abroad except for one trip to Israel in the mid-1970s when our daughters were already teenagers.

We remain close-knit today. Our children have in common a wonderful buoyancy that makes our frequent family gatherings times of merriment and even hilarity. David's sense of humor is probably the most irreverent in the family, but his sisters almost matched him with a skit at his wedding imitating the Spice Girls and roasting his bride, Gina.

They have taken very different paths in life. But our kids all share a strong belief in the need for social justice, feelings that developed when they were youngsters. They have shown sensitivity to the less fortunate and have never chosen to turn away from society's problems. We would have sent any of them to private school, had they wanted that, but each child not only felt more comfortable in the public system but also understood the larger reason for being there. David put it into words, but I know that the girls felt the same way. "I want to be in a school with *all* sorts," he told me when he was a teenager, "because those are the people I'll be living with for the rest of my life."

Eda and I have a similar commitment to public education. Serving the majority of the population, the public schools must maintain high standards. If they decline, our society will be left catering to a privileged few.

Eda and I are on the left celebrating our fiftieth wedding anniversary on a trip to England with extended family in the summer of 2003

We have been progressive in our political and social views in other respects as well, and frequently I have objected to our country's policies. It is criticism that comes from a love of country that only an immigrant can have. I am eternally grateful to America for the refuge it provided and the freedom it has given me. Yet unlike many other Holocaust survivors, especially those who have done well financially, I haven't hesitated to speak my mind when I feel the nation is going down the wrong path.

Some of my dissent stems from a distrust of politicians, whoever they are. During my early years in the States, I was appalled at the military buildup at the beginning of the Cold War and the demonizing of the Soviet Union. Not that the USSR wasn't an oppressive regime and a threat to world peace. I had lived under Stalinism and knew very well the human suffering it caused. But what troubled me was the way our leaders magnified out of all proportion the threat *to us* posed by the Russian bear. They made it seem as if we were in a war to the death with an all-powerful monster of an enemy—and I didn't buy it.

During and after the war I had been an eyewitness to the utter poverty of that country and its reliance on donations of food from America to avoid starvation. The Soviet distribution system was in a hopeless state of malfunction, many of the ethnic groups were embroiled in blood feuds, and even the highly touted Red Army was a lot less potent than you would know by just watching the grand military parades. Yes, it had defeated Hitler, but with help from the Allies and the partisans, from German blunders and the Russian winter. I could see how skilled Stalin's generals were in bluffing, how they had moved squadrons of planes from one airfield to another to give the impression of a great air force. The idea that the Soviets could somehow conquer America was ridiculous. But such fears were fueled by the "military-industrial complex,"

Traveling with Eda

as President Eisenhower called it, which created the myth of a mighty foe to justify the expenditure of billions for armaments.

My disagreement with our arms buildup during the early decades of the Cold War led me to oppose the Korean conflict (which I did not have to fight in due to flat feet) and above all the war in Vietnam, a crusade against communism that I thought was rank stupidity from its inception. What purpose was served by a military adventure, far from our shores, that led to the deaths of almost sixty thousand Americans and an untold number of Vietnamese? I am still bitter toward the architects of that bloodbath and their advisors, the "wise men" from the best schools in the land who with their arrogance and miscalculation did a terrible disservice to our country. And something comparable is unfolding in Iraq today.

In the early eighties Israel stumbled into its own Vietnam—Lebanon—and I reacted the same way. I did not approve of the siege of Beirut that took the lives of so many soldiers and civilians. I am a great booster of the Jewish state and now that I have a daughter and granddaughter living there I feel closer to it than ever before. By any measure, the ingathering of millions of Jews from lands where they've been persecuted is an extraordinary achievement. But every nation makes big mistakes, and Israel is no exception.

As early as 1967, I felt that the occupation of the West Bank and Gaza was a flawed policy. Every effort should have been made to return those territories to Jordan. The government in Jerusalem was shortsighted in thinking it could rule over so large and hostile a population. And then later it made the situation worse by encouraging Jewish settlements—not merely in strategic locations but willy-nilly across the area—that required more in the way of an armed presence. Even if it had been necessary to take over the territories, Israel should have used all the resources at its disposal to raise the standard of living of the Palestinians, getting them "invested" in stability and peace. It's common sense that if people are deprived of adequate water, housing, and education they are going to hate you, and the miserable refugee camps naturally evolved as breeding grounds for terrorists.

Now things have reached a point where reconciliation may no longer be possible, and it is hard for me to foresee Arafat or any of his successors accepting Israel's existence within *any* boundaries. In fact, the whole Arab world would destroy Israel if it could. I do not have a solution of my own to offer; more than anything else I'm fearful about the safety of my loved ones there and saddened at the thought that peace in the region will likely not be achieved in my lifetime.

But I am also worried about the future of the Jews in America. My wary nature tells me that because of the great heights we have attained in business and the professions, politics and the media, we could be riding for a hard fall. I've studied the case of the Jews of late medieval Spain who rose to the top of the ladder only to be knocked off. And even before that, England and France expelled their Jewish communities. The best modern example, of course, is German Jewry before Hitler, a community that produced many leading figures in science, journalism, and the arts, and felt secure—in some cases, even after Nazism came to power.

I know all the arguments about America being different, and I agree that we are protected against tyranny by our centuries-old constitution. But it can be overridden in times of crisis, as we saw in the fall of 2001 when the government appropriated sweeping emergency powers. Even the coexistence of our country's ethnic groups is something I view as a fragile compact. I have witnessed neighbors killing neighbors in Eastern Europe and know how suddenly mass savagery can erupt. The race riots in Los Angeles and Crown Heights that shocked us in the past decade are proof that it *can* happen here.

There was nothing even in my background, however, to prepare me for September 11. Despite everything I had been exposed to in the war, until I saw those towers come down, I had never encountered such a massive destruction of life in one blow. But I experienced none of the loss of innocence that so many other Americans felt. For me it was only further evidence that the world is a jungle. And the anti-Zionism and anti-Semitism in the wake of the attack, a lot of it on college campuses, make me even more nervous about the security of the Jews in this country. My kids are not so apprehensive and they don't feel this kind of uneasiness in the United States. But given what I've been through, I will never feel truly comfortable anywhere.

My concern about the danger lurking out there has affected the direction of our philanthropy. We support many different things, ranging from Jewish organizations such as the Federation and its Endowment Fund and the Osher Marin Jewish Community Center, to general causes such as the YMCA, the San Francisco Museum of Modern Art, and the research and treatment of cancer. But we care most deeply about Holocaust studies. We have under-written graduate fellowships at the Hebrew University of Jerusa-lem for the study of the roots of the Shoah, supported courses on the Holocaust for future priests and ministers at the Graduate Theological Union, and endowed a program that annually brings a visiting scholar on the subject to UC Berkeley. Recently, Eda came up with the idea of an entire course comparing the Spanish Inquisition with the Holocaust. We have sponsored it for several years at Lehrhaus Judaica—the Bay Area's largest school for adult Jewish education, of which Eda was the first president—and it has always drawn a big turnout.

We want people to think seriously about certain recurrent pat-terns of Jewish history over the last two thousand years. Why has almost every era and every country been infected with the virus of anti-Semitism? What has been the role of the Church? Of eco-nomic conditions? Of political opportunism? And how have the Jews themselves responded? If again and again they have been lulled into a false sense of security, what threw them off the mark? Could even ignorance about past events have been a cause of their passivity? It pains me to think that when my family and countless others were making life and death decisions in Poland during the war, our historical perspective, and that of our communal leaders, was so narrow.

Eda and I are realistic enough to know that shedding light on such topics may not prevent another episode of genocide. But we believe that research and teaching in this field—far more vital than reparations, memorials, or museums—is the only hope we have left.

Epilogue

IN 1993, I WAS READY TO RETURN to my native land after nearly half a century. Foreign vacations sometimes tried my patience,
and I hadn't traveled abroad often, but this was different. Nearing
seventy, recently becoming a grandfather, and finally having the
time for study and reflection, I hoped that the journey would help
me face my past.

We went as participants on a two-week study tour of Poland,
the Czech Republic, and Hungary conducted by Lehrhaus Judaica
that included a course with a lot of reading beforehand. Among a
group of almost fifty participants, Eda and I were the only survivors, and it meant a lot to us that at least two of our kids, Debbie
and David, could come along for emotional support.

The three countries on our itinerary had all emerged from the
shadows of Soviet domination only a few years earlier. The mood
we found, especially among the young people, was decidedly
upbeat. In the warm sunshine of late August, the large medieval
town square of Cracow was packed with Western tourists. Brand

new five-star hotels had gone up in Prague. And outside Budapest we visited a bustling resort town overlooking the romantic Danube. But the tour also included three death camps—Auschwitz/Birkenau, Maidanek, and Treblinka—as well as the site of the Warsaw ghetto, and a giant cemetery nearby where the bodies of Jews had been thrown into unmarked graves. In Lublin, we walked through the building that had housed one of the greatest Yeshivas of Europe; it was now a medical school with hardly a trace of its past. At every turn it seemed, the formerly "captive nations" of Eastern Europe were getting a new lease on life, but clearly it was too late for our people whose presence had been almost completely erased. We learned that in the entire country of Poland, which had over three million Jews when I was a boy, perhaps five to ten thousand remained, most of them elderly and poor. In Warsaw, the second-largest Jewish community in the world in 1939, only one synagogue was now functioning. The Germans had stayed its demolition because they used it as a stable.

I became even more upset when I saw that most of the other Jewish landmarks still standing in that part of Europe were now tasteless tourist attractions. Crowds of sightseers, with little knowledge or reverence, elbowed their way into age-old shuls and traipsed over layers of the dead in cemeteries. Prague was the worst, where the haunting Jewish quarter evoked by Kafka resembled Disneyland with mobs of spectators jostling one another in long lines. In Poland, interest in Jewish folklore and emblems like the Star of David had become the latest fad. It reminded me of the fascination with Native American artifacts in the United States. First a people is destroyed, then its symbols are worn as jewelry. I was disturbed, too, by the way Auschwitz was commercialized. The first thing you see is a parking lot full of tour buses, carrying hordes of day-trippers. I felt that they were attracted out of a morbid curiosity rather than a true desire to mourn the dead or ponder the meaning of a place where a million and a half Jews and hundreds of thousands of others had been gassed and cremated. This is a weird form of entertainment, not education, I thought, because one needs to be prepared in mind and spirit before encountering the barracks and gas chambers. How many of these visitors had read even one book on the subject? What had they learned in school about it? And then another contradiction hit me: How ironic that people the world over now come here in droves. Where was the whole world when the greatest crime in history was being committed on this spot? No one lifted a finger to stop it *then*, but now everyone wants to come and gawk.

Few tourists ever make it to Biala Podlaska, of course, which we reached on our own side trip after a two-hour taxi ride from Warsaw. I was surprised by the lack of progress in fifty years. There was a lot of construction going on when we arrived, but it was for installing an underground sewer system for the first time. Only now was the small city getting indoor plumbing. The pretty main square with its chestnut trees was still there, and it reminded Eda of the Northern California town of Sonoma where a park in the center is lined with shops. But the busy clothing and jewelry establishments I remembered as a kid had never been revived. There were just a few food stores and an ice cream shop instead, and a public toilet. Nearby I noted the spot from which the bus used to depart for its daily run to Warsaw. Several blocks away we passed the sites of my father's butcher shop and his synagogue. Both had been torn down.

We started to walk toward my old neighborhood. The first thing I noticed was the communal pump from which I had drawn water every day. It had been moved from one side of the street to

The water pump that I remember from my childhood.

the other but looked to me like the same contraption. And then
we turned the corner onto Ulica Yatkova. My house at number 14
was no longer there. Probably because it had been on a big lot, it
was the one sacrificed to make way for a plain, squat office building. Otherwise the block was little changed. Across the street, the
Piekarnia bakery that had heated our midday Shabbes meals during my childhood was still in operation.

Directly opposite where my former home had been, I noticed
an identical house, a fourplex with the same stairway going up to
the second floor. I explained to Eda, Debbie, and David how my
family had lived on one side of the hall and my aunt and uncle and
their two daughters had occupied the unit across from ours.

As we stood on the sidewalk, an old Polish woman came out
and stared at us suspiciously. Unnerved by our Western clothing,
our conspicuous cameras, and the English we spoke among our-

selves, she soon launched into a tirade about the suffering of the Poles during the war. It may have been that she feared we had returned to lay claim to her house. Others on the street turned their heads and looked at us with a mixture of curiosity and contempt.

For the first time since 1944 I had come back to the town of my birth, to the block where I had been raised, and the old hatred still seemed to be there. Now as then, I felt it best not to reveal my identity. But I did engage the lady in conversation. "When did you come here?" I asked in my rusty Polish. "1940," she answered, and I realized how soon that was after six hundred Jews, including my family, had fled Biala Podlaska and the Nazis had occupied the town. And what, I wanted to know, had happened to Ulica Yatkova 14? "No idea," she said and then continued to jabber on

With David on Ulica Yatkova

defiantly about how everything had been the fault of the Germans and not the Poles. I would have preferred to continue this a little longer and see something of her house and yard, but a few rough-looking men emerged from behind the building and lumbered toward us with menacing expressions on their faces. The four of us backed away quickly and went to our taxi. I told the driver to head out of the residential section of town and toward the riverbank.

Eventually we reached the bridge, got out, and walked over to the point from which as a kid I had jumped down and come up swimming. The water level was very low now—perhaps due to a scarcity of rainfall that summer—and we all got a good chuckle out of that because I had told them the story many times and it obviously depended on a deep river. But I recognized the place all right, and I thought of a boy who grew up in this town. He was small, quiet, and sometimes painfully shy but willing to take risks.

As a nine-year-old, from this very spot, I had taken a leap into the unknown, an act of faith not in any other person or in the heavens above, but in myself. Looking at the laughing faces of my wife and children around me and thinking of the life and career I had made on a distant shore in the shadow of another bridge, I realized how far that leap had been.

Afterword and Acknowledgments

JOE PELL IS A RETICENT MAN who first gave me an inkling of his life story while we were traveling together in East-Central Europe on a Lehrhaus Judaica study tour that I led in 1993. The last evening of the trip, in Budapest, he and Eda invited me to dinner to mark the end of our intense journey. In response to my questions, he quietly related how his entire family had been murdered by the Nazis, and how he had fled to the forest, joined a partisan brigade, and fought back. Although I had read many Holocaust memoirs, something about Joe's experience and the unvarnished way he recounted it singularly moved, informed, and ultimately uplifted me. I hoped his personal history could be preserved.

In 1999, during another Lehrhaus trip, in the friendlier environs of New York City, we visited the new Museum of Jewish Heritage—A Living Memorial to the Holocaust. Viewing the core exhibition covering several floors of galleries, Joe was visibly upset with the paucity of material on the Jewish resistance to the

Germans. During the next few days he spoke to me about his desire to write a book.

What followed was about two dozen taped interviews with Joe at his home, each between three and four hours long. I transcribed them and, using his words as the core of the text, shaped the foregoing narrative. He read the manuscript numerous times, correcting me when I had misunderstood his meaning and adding material that he recalled after our conversations. Reliving the traumatic moments of his youth was a painful process for Joe, but one he endured not only for the edification of his family and friends but also for the sake of adding to the historical record of those times. I will always admire him for delving into his past with such candor and courage.

I interviewed some individuals who knew Joe before he immigrated to America, most notably Noah Rodzinek, from Biala Podlaska, whom I tracked down in Queens, New York. This project brought him and Joe together for the first time in almost sixty years. I was privileged to be at their reunion and taped the encounter. But most of my research was conducted in libraries and archives. Especially useful were the two memorial books of Biala Podlaska (1953 and 1961), available at the Dorot Jewish Division of the New York Public Library, and I thank Judy Fixler of that institution for cheerfully helping me translate the Yiddish text. I was also assisted in putting Joe's early years into context by excellent studies such as Norman Salsitz' *A Jewish Boyhood in Poland* (1992), Theo Richmond's *Konin* (1995), and Celia Heller's classic *On the Edge of Destruction* (1977).

For the four wartime chapters of this book, I was aided immensely by Shmuel Spector's well-researched *Holocaust of Volhynian Jews, 1941–1944* (1990) and Reuben Ainsztein's comprehensive *Jewish Resistance in Nazi-occupied Eastern Europe* (1975). I also gained much from Nechama Tec's *Defiance: The Bielski Partisans* (1993), her *Resilience and Courage: Men, Women and the Holocaust* (2003), and Primo Levi's evocative novel, *If Not Now, When?* (1985). The three volumes of memoirs by Jozef Sobiesiak, Joe's partisan commander, exist only in Polish, and key passages were translated for me by Andrzej Salski, a Warsaw journalist residing in Berkeley. I am also grateful to Joseph Voss of Seattle, an energetic, independent scholar on the partisans of Volhynia, for his valuable insights and for the useful material he sent me, including many detailed maps of the region. Through Mr. Voss, I was able to contact another historian of the Jewish resistance in the Manievich area, Jack Nusan Porter of the University of Massachusetts at Lowell, whose two sisters were killed in the massacre of September 4, 1942, and whose parents fought in Kruk's brigade. Jack's mother, Fay Porter, graciously consented to a telephone interview with me. For the postliberation period, which has received far too little scholarly attention, I relied upon sources such as the *American Jewish Yearbook* for the mid-1940s, Yehuda Bauer's *Flight and Rescue: Bricha* (1970), and the revealing memoir of Samuel Pisar, *Of Blood and Hope* (1980). For the last third of the book, Joe's life in California since 1947, I was helped by a number of works, particularly Walter B. Helmreich's perceptive *Against all Odds* (1992), on the successful lives many survivors made in America. I also drew upon the research I had myself conducted for several books on Bay Area Jewish history. Joe, too, read long excerpts from all of the above secondary sources, which I sent him during the course of our collaboration. Discussing that literature with him was among the most rewarding aspects of this project.

Along with Eda and the four Pell children—Debra, Karen, Becky, and David—many individuals read this manuscript in draft. Joe and I thank them for their suggestions and encouragement:

Seymour Fromer, David Biale, Dr. Steven Frankel, Ken and Julie Cohen, Harold Lindenthal, Elizabeth Hansot, my sister Bobbi Leigh Zito, and my lifelong partner Dorothy Shipps.

The book was edited by the talented Don DeNevi, who helped me configure the overall structure of the story and taught me a great deal about writing in the process. I am also grateful to Bob Drews and Sunah Cherwin for their copyediting and proofreading and to Sara Glaser for her outstanding design of the volume.

Above all, Joe and I thank Eda. We benefited from her good judgment and intellectual curiosity every step of the way.

Fred Rosenbaum